TESTIMONIALS
ONCE UPON A RHYME

"Just when you think John O'Connor has reminisced about everything that was great about football in the old days, his next poem reminds you of another thing that you loved about the game back then. Once Upon a Rhyme in Football is unapologetically nostalgic but O'Connor's wit, personality and deep love for the game bring everything he writes about to bright new life. These conversational poems – born on the terraces, in the pub and around the grounds – are for everybody who's ever enjoyed football."

—Liam Drew: Writer – journalist and author of
I, Mammal: The story of what makes us Mammals

"John's wonderful book is like leafing through the poetical equivalent of an old Football Sticker Album. Every piece sparking a fond memory of the way football used to be and the colourful characters that inhabited that bygone age. An important book, rich in humour, insight and observations about our favourite game – both as it was and what it has become. Essential reading for any football fan."

—Neil Witherow: author of
Don't mention The 'SPOR and former editor of *Palace-Echo*

"John O'Connor's evocative poetry will strike a chord with all those supporters who can remember when football really was the Beautiful Game. His poems both poignant and powerful, are like a snippet of BACKPASS magazine in verse. We love them… long live the good old days."

—Mike Berry:
editor of *BACKPASS*, the retro football magazine

Once Upon a Rhyme in FOOTBALL

Crystal Palace goalkeeper John Jackson, celebrating David Payne's equalizer against West Ham, at Upton Park in 1972.

Photo attribution. Tower Hamlets studios.

Once Upon a Rhyme in FOOTBALL

NOSTALGIC SOCCER STORIES
IN VERSE OR WORSE

John J. O'Connor

"A feast of fun, sharp comment and memorable characters."

Table of Contents

Introduction	xiii
1. Reminicences	1
2. A Vanished Breed (The Scottish Winger)	4
3. A Thunderbolt Strikes In Heaven	8
4. Where Have All the Great Captain Gone?	10
5. You Can Smoke Now Up In Heaven	13
6. You're Fired	17
7. Mr. Chairman You're 'Avin a Larf	19
8. Arise Sir Steve	26
9. Football Farm (Part One)	29
10. Big Pat From the County Down	34
11. Harry's Greatest Saves	38
12. "Don't Get Me Wrong"	40
13. West Germany's and Montezuma's Revenge	44
14. Bertie Hislop No Man's Land Hero	50
15. Football Farm (Part Two) Football Birds	59
16. Crystal Palace Memories (1969-79)	63
17. Good-Bye to the Terrace	73
18. King's Road King	75

19.	The Proud Preston Plumber	77
20.	The Bootroom Up In Heaven	81
21.	Tactical Error	89
22.	The Year 16	92
23.	The Taming of Wayne (He's Only 19) Rooney	95
24.	They're Wearing Cricket Pads In Heaven	103
25.	Bobby Kellard (He Was Well - Ard)	105
26.	Bob – The Man From the V.A.R.	107
27.	There's Only One Banksy	112
28.	The Nouveau Football Fan	115
29.	Away Alone at CIT-EH	119
30.	Football Quiz Nite Down the Pub	127
31.	Having A.ball In Heaven	133
32.	Football Victim	136
33.	Geographical Football	140
34.	To Hell or to Orient!	143
35.	A Little Pub In Scotland	147
36.	Football Occupations	148
37.	Eliminate the Hyphenate	151
38.	Mrs. Minchella (The Palace Peanut Sella)	153
39.	We Want Whittle	161
40.	Ham – Burg 0-0 West – Ham	164
41.	Dirty Tricks and Celery Sticks	167
42.	Football Farm Part 3: Football In the Water	169
43.	Give Tuesday Night a Break	172
44.	Players Profiles (Past and Present)	175

45. Mixing Football and Religion	182
46. John The Shovel - Sewell An Awfully Civilized Defender	186
47. A Dream of Two 'Alves	188
48. An Old Ex-Pro's Lament	191
49. The Old Man and His Grandson	194
50. The Night My Mum Killed Bobby Charlton	201
51. "Now That George Best Fella Was a Great Fella" R.I.P. Dad	207
Afterword	213
Acknowledgements	215
About the Author	217

THE GAME OF FOOTBALL WAS DESIGNED TO KEEP COAL MINERS OFF THE STREETS.

— Jimmy Breslin

Introduction

Like a lot of football fans around my age I yearn for the good old days, when players took public transport, lived in the manor and were approachable when you saw them down the local pub the night before a match. Sure, players are faster and fitter now; pitches are like bowling greens and fans sit down quietly, rarely get rowdy, and have no problem strolling back to their seats with a pizza ten minutes into the second half. All very civilized – but come on, admit it, wasn't it better back in the day?

Of course, it was. So, if you're expecting this book to be a shrine to Rio Ferdinand, Gareth Bale, John Terry, or the MK Dons, you'll be sorely disappointed. In the same breath, if you're expecting the poetic style of Wordsworth or even Dylan Thomas you might be better off going to the bookshop's poetry section. What I have created is a collection of football stories about players, managers, fans, and memorable events associated with the game.

Now don't let the word poem frighten you off. I know it might not do your well-earned street cred any good, when you tell your mates down the pub that you have just invested in a book of poetry. But not to worry, these footballing stories, written in a narrative form of rhyme are not full of deep meanings which might require you to invest in a shipment of psychedelic drugs to decipher. A pint of lager and a couple of packets of crisps should be a sufficient companion when you enjoy these tales of yore.

Some of these tales might give you a chuckle, some move you to shed a tear. We have a good-natured laugh at VAR, the modern chairman and the nouveau football fan. Among the 51 stories are memories of the 1970 World Cup, the demise of the Scottish winger and the toxicity of travelling to away games in the 1970's. There's also stories of courageous goalkeepers; some diving at the feet of forwards and one diving into a burning plane. All in the name of making a save. Also, you'll read of the brave warriors who played football on the muddy fields of France and Belgium during The Great War. For many of them, it was the last ball they'd ever kick.

The Rest in Peace poems should not be taken as morbid but as a celebration of the lives of these footballing greats. Some of the other yarns can be taken with an extra handful of sodium extract. However, the one thing they all do is recall the way the great game used to be and how a great many of us wish it still was. Hope you enjoy.

John J. O'Connor

REMINISCENCES

As I lay down on my couch
I start to reminisce
And I start to make a note,
Of all the things I miss.
Like the Golden Age of football,
An era that's gone by
When goalkeepers could catch the ball
And wingers they could fly.

I miss Law, Best, and Charlton
'The Holy Trinity,'
And up the road at City
Lee, Bell, and Summerbee.
I miss the 'School of Science'
Harvey, Kendall, Ball
And the Liverpool intelligentsia
Steve Heighway – Brian Hall.

There were some real hard cases,
Compared to nowadays
The likes of Stiles and Tommy Smith
Would have terrified the Krays.
Sure, the players today are fitter
And they run around much faster
But they're pumped up full of nutrients
And force-fed plates of pasta.
They also love to show
Their abs off when they score

Once Upon a Rhyme in Football

Find the nearest puddle
And slide along the floor.

Yes, I miss the Scottish wingers
And the crosses they supplied
You never had a hope in hell
Without one in your side.
I miss the terrace surge
And the chanting of the crowd
And the mighty Kop at Liverpool
Where they sang 'Walk On' out loud.
Yes, I miss the player's chewing gum
And spitting on the floor
I miss the North Bank Highbury
And the deafening Roker Roar.
No, things will never be the same,
That's for bloody sure
As I remember big Martin Chivers,
Joe Royle and Bobby Moore.
Watching the likes of Pogba
Having a non-stop moan
Where art thou Jim Montgomery
Where are you Dick Malone?
So good luck to the Premiership,
Where everyone's a star
But I still yearn for the good old days
And the likes of Willie Carr.

In the opening poem I mentioned our good friend the Scottish winger. Many of us who followed football before the Sky television revolution can recall some of those wizards on the wing. Yes, some of them could be cantankerous little bastards, but boy, could they get the crowd going? You bet they could.

With socks usually around their ankles, they'd taunt the full back with an array of skills perfected after thousands of hours of practice on the cobbled streets of urban Scotland. Once finished with the teasing, they'd glide past the unfortunate full back (who'd usually be described in the press the next day as cumbersome) and send over a cross for a usually large brute of an old-fashioned English centre forward.

The likes of Jimmy Johnstone, Willie Henderson, Charlie Cooke and Eddy Gray could change the course of a game with a little dip of the shoulder and a swivel of the hips. Unfortunately, though, like the whistling milkman and the friendly bus conductor the Scottish wing men are players of the past. Possession football and all that ticky-tacky, passy – passy, Barcelona stuff has made them redundant.

Jimmy (Jinky) Johnstone of Celtic and Scotland in action against England. (ALAMY)

A VANISHED BREED
(the Scottish winger)

They couldn't produce goalkeepers
And Andy Stewart couldn't sing.
But what Bonny Scotland could produce
Was wizards on the wing.
The home of great inventors
Of engineers and thrift
The players they turned out on the wing
Became English football's gift.

They were described as feisty, canny
As fiery – nippy – wee
The likes of them, unfortunately
Again, we'll never see.
Yes, those magic little gentlemen
Filled Scottish hearts with pride
But the Scottish winger has disappeared
Like the shipyards on the Clyde.

'Twas places like the Gorbals,
And the close-knit mining towns
That reared these little geniuses
To make full backs look like clowns.
Poverty had made some look
As if they suffered malnutrition
But feed them the ball out on the wing
And you witnessed a magician
Dribbling from the tenements

John J. O'Connor

Ball glued fast to the feet
And treating every lamp-post
As if it was a man to beat.
Learning to dip the shoulder
And dummy the defender;
Weaving with the tennis ball
Like a drunk out on a bender.

Then when they got to fifteen years
With potential not in doubt
They were whisked south of the border
By an English football scout.
Then despite the language barrier
And the pain of being home-sick
After building up on English steak
They became a first team pick.

As they would stroll along the touchline,
Shins exposed by lowered socks
They'd aim to reach the bye-line
And then produce a cross.
Yes, most were temperamental
And could easily throw a looper
But will Scotland ever produce again
The likes of Davie Cooper?
Now the Glasgow lamp-post is all alone
Except for the lone canine
And street football is finito
Cos the kids are all on-line

Once Upon a Rhyme in Football

East Enders starts at eight o'clock
So there's no one on the street
Except the ghosts of the old wingmen
With magic in their feet.

Many of us are at the age where we attend more funerals than weddings and get drunk at more wakes than stag parties. We're coming to the time in life where a lot of those wonderful players, whose pictures we had plastered all over our bedroom walls, are being taken to the big pitch in the sky. Peter Lorimer, Leeds United's great Scottish winger was one of those. He passed away in March 2021. That great Leeds team of the late 60's and early 70's was decimated in just 15 months. Between April 2020 and July 2021, the Whites lost Norman Hunter, Trevor Cherry, Jack Charlton, Mick Bates, Terry Cooper and of course, Peter himself.

Famed for his ferocious shot, Lorimer was the youngest player to debut for the Leeds first team. He was an unorthodox winger who liked nothing better than cutting inside and testing out the goalkeeper with one of his blistering shots. Nicknamed Thunder Boots, between 1962 and 1985 he amassed more than 500 league games for the Peacocks and scored 238 goals in all competitions.

He was also capped 21 times for Scotland and appeared in the 1974 World Cup in West Germany. Lorimer was also a formidable penalty taker, although I do recall him having one saved by a goalie called Dickie Guy in an FA cup tie against non-league Wimbledon back in '75.

I'm sure upstairs there's a lot of saints and probably a few sinners who've sneaked in, ducking for cover when, as commentators would say, "Lorimer is about to unleash one."

A THUNDERBOLT STRIKES THROUGH THE CLOUDS

The strike of a thunderbolt
Blasts past Heaven's Gates
And God says to Jack Charlton
"'ere's one of your mates.
I know Trevor and Norman
will be both happy too,"
As he nods to Saint Peter
To let Lorimer through.
"There's a place for you, Peter lad,
out there on that wing.
Now be easy with your shooting
cos your shots don't 'arf sting."

So, he met with his Leeds team-mates
And they reminisced of the past
As Revie gazed proudly
At Peter having a blast.

So Rest in Peace to the Scotsman
With the right foot of great power
That terrified the free-kick walls
And made goalkeepers cower.

Along with the wingman another attribute that seems to have disappeared is the strong personality of team captains. There are exceptions of course, with the lad Rice at West Ham having the potential to be a great captain. One thing I've noticed though is that modern footballers, despite their impressive skills and fitness levels, do not make great captains. They seem to lack the leadership qualities that make a man stand out among men. Some of the born captains of the past may not have been their team's best player. Many of them would have had no hesitation in liberating the ball from an opponent with a perfectly timed two footed tackle from behind. But they commanded the respect of their managers and team-mates alike. They led by example and were usually the conduit between the gaffers and the lads in the dressing room.

The great Dave Mackay. A man amongst men. (Press Association)

Watching matches in recent seasons I've wondered where the hell's the captain? Where is the man with his sleeves rolled up, urging on his team-mates? I've even witnessed a captain, who was also the club's penalty-taker, having the ball snatched out of his hands and the kick taken by some prima donna who wanted to get his name on the score sheet to boost his confidence, ego, arrogance – whatever you want to call it. Or the refusal of Chelsea goalkeeper Kepa Arrizabalaga to be substituted in extra time of the 2019 League Cup final against Manchester City. I mean where was the captain to give him a swift kick up the behind to help him on his way to the touchline? If any of these spoilt brat antics were tried with old school skippers like McLintock, Blanchflower or Mackay, the culprit would be eating his nutri-balanced dinner through a straw for the foreseeable future.

WHERE HAVE ALL THE CAPTAINS GONE?

Organizing – Pointing – Shouting Man – On
Where have all great Captains gone?
Urging–Goading – heart on sleeve,
When did all the great Captains leave?

Clenched fist rollickings at those lapsi-daisy
Calming players who are acting crazy.
Always sporting if they lost or won…
Oh where have all the great Captains gone?

John J. O'Connor

Memories of Bremner and Mackay
For the cause prepared to die
Bobby Moore and Chopper Ron
Oh where have all the great Captains gone?

It's not just wing men and captains who have disappeared from the modern game. Modern managers do not possess the personality that made so many of the old school gaffers such loveable characters.

Sure, Kloppy is everyone's favourite German and Pep seems like a nice bloke, but come on, who would you rather hang out with for a night? These two talking about the pressing game, fine margins, and the need to warm down, or Cloughie, Shankly and Redknapp talking about any subject under the moon while putting the world to rights at the same time? If I had to pick an ex-manager to share a cocktail with, it would be the character that the descriptions larger than life, flamboyant and charismatic had been specially invented for. The next poem is about that character.

Sadly, Big Malcolm Allison passed away in 2010. After a playing career cut short by tuberculosis, he made a name for himself as an innovative assistant to Manchester City's then manager Joe Mercer. Next, he gained legendary status during his three-year reign as the controversial and eccentric manager of Crystal Palace.

As a lifelong Palace fan I was particularly hard hit by his death. I thought back to the winter of 1976 when Big Mal, with the customary cigar, sheepskin coat and fedora, took Palace fans on the trip of their lifetime. On that journey he steered Third Division Crystal Palace to the semi-final of the FA Cup. We, his disciples had so much faith in the Messiah that if a tsunami had been forecast in South London we'd have probably got up and legged it, safe in the knowledge that the Big Man himself would be able to walk his way over the water to safety.

We lost that semi-final game to the eventual winners Southampton, but the memories of that Cup run and Big Mal's part in it will never be forgotten. Along the Cup trail we not only won at places like Leeds, Chelsea and Sunderland but also played those teams off the

*Big Mal, with the customary cigar and champagne,
on the train returning from Sunderland in 1976.*

park. For a few months, we owned the back pages of the tabloids and everyone who followed our Messiah on that journey will never forget it. Thanks for the magical trip Big Mal. R.I.P. Messiah!

YOU CAN SMOKE NOW UP IN HEAVEN

The No Smoking signs in heaven
Have been taken down today
As God informs St Peter
That Big Mal is on his way.

"We'll have to bend the rules a bit
This man has such an aura.
Find a cloud for his sheepskin coat
And a hook for his fedora.
Also, Pete, when you get a chance
Will you ice up the champagne?
I've a feeling the heaven that we know
Will never be the same.
The women angels they'll flock to him,
Of that you can be sure
And I believe that news has already reached
The ears of Bobby Moore.
Already down in earth-dom
He's been mourned in towns and shires
And especially in South London,
Where they called him "The Messiah."
Warn him of his language Pete,
He's known as quite a curser
And to make him feel much more at home
Put him next to old Joe Mercer
Let them coach the coming match,
The derby game v Hell
Remember that these two coached
Lee, Summerbee and Bell."
So Big Mal lands up in heaven
And he doesn't miss a beat
As he tells God to "move over,
I think you're in my seat.

John J. O'Connor

You've been up here forever
it's a feat I do admire
But one thing to remember God
THERE'S ONLY ONE MESSIAH."

Mind you, Big Mal did well by Chairman Ray Bloye at Palace. How many modern chairmen would watch their teams drop two divisions in two seasons, fail to win promotion from the Third division with a team who were on First Division wages, and still have faith in the manager? Not a lot I would think. How many modern chairmen would see pictures in the daily rag of Malcolm arriving to training straight from a night club with soft porn star Fiona Richmond in tow and brush it off as Malcolm being Malcolm? Not very many.

To make matters worse (or funnier, depending on your sense of humour) pictures also appeared of the divine Miss Richmond topless with the players in the communal bath. Ray Bloye, despite calls for Malcolm's head from some Puritan directors, had great patience. He saw the funny side .And under the spell of the Messiah he couldn't pull the trigger.

Patience like that, is a virtue seldom practiced any more, especially among some of the newbie owners. Many of them are oligarchs or tycoons who don't seem to understand the culture of the product they have invested in. Then you have the local wide boys who made fortunes from the likes of flogging mobile phones when they first became mainstream. They might have made millions, but outside their special fields they are mostly unknown to the general public. Once they buy a club they become famous and their egos go into over-drive. Very few have the well-being of the clubs or the fans at heart. They look at the football grounds as potential blocks of luxury flats. And after a poor run of results, they'll thank the manager for all he has done for the club, explain to the media that the game is a results-driven business, then appoint a new manager – one they've quietly been negotiating with for months. Yes, I think if Big Mal was around now, after the first relegation he'd be hearing the words of the next poem's title.

YOU'RE FIRED

They said I lost the room
Where all the players dressed
Thanked me for all my efforts
And wished me all the best
My replacement then appeared
Just minutes past my sacking
And only two days after the Board
Had given me their backing.
They said – unlike the local grocer
I could not set my stall
And that football's a results-based industry
So I had to take the fall.
I'll now go about my gardening leave,

And I'll spend time with the wife,
Take more coaching badges
And get away from stress and strife.
I'll rid my eyes of their sleepless bags
And my hair of gray I'll dye
And before I ply my trade again,
I'll work a bit for Sky.
Then I'll go abroad to coach a while,
To boost my resume
Come back next early season
When my options I will weigh.
They said I left a bitter man
When they gave me my termination
In that there is no grain of truth
Though I wish them relegation
So let them find their dressing room
And re-arrange their stall
Park the bus where the hell they want
   AND I HOPE THEY WIN F-ALL

It's not all one-way traffic though. Sometimes it's the manager who has the last laugh at the expense of the chairman. Plenty of managers with airtight contracts have been quite happy to work in the back yard and listen to the missus telling them where she wants her daffodils planted. Meanwhile they cash in huge cheques for the remainder of their lucrative contract. A contract the chairman gladly watched them sign. Basically, every time they stroll up to their local bank branch, they're 'avin' a larf.'

MR CHAIRMAN – YOU'RE 'AVIN' A LARF

"I'm giving a vote of confidence
to both you and your staff."

"OH, COME ON MR CHAIRMAN,
YOU MUST BE 'AVIN' A LARF."

"You'll have the overwhelming backing,
of myself and all the Board
and if you need some transfer funds,
we'll make sure we can afford."

"HA, HA MR CHAIRMAN
YOU'RE FIBBING ME – NOT 'ARF.
COME ON MR CHAIRMAN,
YOU'RE 'AVIN' A BLOODY LARF."

"I'm looking to the long term
I don't expect instant success
I'll protect you from the rage of fans

And rumours in the press.
I won't interfere in team affairs,
I'll let you have free reign
but I'd like if you'd play Enrique,
the kid I signed from Spain."

"HE DIVED FIVE TIMES ON HIS DEBUT,
THEN GOT SENT FOR AN EARLY BATH
COME ON MR CHAIRMAN,
YOU MUST BE 'AVIN' A LARF."

"He's only on twenty grand a week,
which is a lot less dough than Rob
and football nowadays
is about trying to save a bob."

"YOUNG ROB HE'LL PLAY FOR ENGLAND,
HE EVEN PLAYED WITH A BUSTED CALF
COME ON MR CHAIRMAN,
YOU'RE 'AVIN' A BLOODY LARF"

"I think the squad we have right now
is good enough to keep us up
and I don't want you to play the first team
in that stupid FA Cup."

"BUT WE COULD GET TO THE CUP FINAL
AND TO EUROPE – IT'S A PATH
OH COME ON MR CHAIRMAN
YOU MUST BE 'AVIN' A LARF."

John J. O'Connor

"I'm going to look for some investors
a Russian or a Yank
I don't care if they don't know football
as long as they've money in the bank."

"YOU KNOW THE FANS WON'T LIKE IT
YOU TREAT 'EM LIKE THEY'RE DAFT
COME ON MR CHAIRMAN
YOU'VE GOT TO BE 'AVIN A LARF."

"I've only got an interest,
in fans who own club stocks
and the ones each match who wine and dine
in my luxury private box."

"YEAH THE ONES WHO EAT PRAWN COCKTAILS
AND DRINK WINE INSTEAD OF DRAUGHT
OH COME ON MR CHAIRMAN,
YOU MUST BE 'AVIN' A LARF."

"I've just this moment changed my mind,
I need a more scientific approach.
So I no longer need your services
as my manager and coach.
I'll hire a foreign gentleman
with an exotic sounding name.
The media will love him
and his continental game.
He'll come in with sexy tactics
do away with the British graft

So sod off, Mister Manager
while I go and have a LARF."

"AH, REMEMBER JUST LAST YEAR
WHEN WE WENT UP TO THE PREM?
AND YOU TOLD ME AS A MANAGER
I WAS A BLOODY GEM.
AS WE BOTH GOT DRUNK OUT OF THE CUP
YOU SAID I WAS THE BEST COACH
YOU'D EVER SAW
AND YOU MADE ME SIGN A CONTRACT
UNTIL TWENTY-TWENTY FOUR
SO I'LL SIT OUT IN MY GARDEN
AND PRACTICE MY GARDENING CRAFT
AND WHEN I CASH MY CHEQUE EACH WEEK
IT WILL BE ME 'AVIN" A LARF."

John J. O'Connor

One of the toughest jobs in football management is the England job. For an English-born football manager, steering the national side is held to be the pinnacle of ambition. It does, however, seem more like a poisoned chalice that has destroyed the reputation of many a good manager. Don Revie, who built the great Leeds team, was announced in 1974 as Sir Alf Ramsey's successor as England manager with great fanfare from the press. Three years later he was made public enemy number one because he had the cheek to quit the job and take up a position in the United Arab Emirates before the old farts at London's Soho Square could have the satisfaction of firing him. They did get to charge him though with 'bringing the game into disrepute.'

Don Revie and wife Elsie arrive in London for his High Court battle with the FA. (Syndication International)

In the 80's Bobby Robson was often pathologically hounded by the Fleet Street keyboard bashers. Robson's treatment was mild compared with what awaited his successor, Graham Taylor. Known to be one of the nicest men in football, after a defeat by Sweden, Taylor was subjected to what became known as the turnip campaign. His head was superimposed on a turnip by The Sun newspaper, for all the nation to laugh at. Forever more in the lower echelons of journalism, he was known as Turnip Head. Later, the likes of Glenn Hoddle and Steve McClaren were forced out of what became known as football's most cursed job. A fly on the wall documentary called "An Impossible Job" was released in 1994 and really destroyed the legacy of some of those in it.

Steve McClaren, who managed England from 2006-07, will forever be known as the "Wally with the Brolly" for having the audacity to stand in the pouring rain, on the sidelines at Wembley in 2007 holding an umbrella over his head. England lost to Croatia that night and McClaren was vilified by the press.

You do wonder though, if England had won would the press have been lauding him for how cool he looked under his fashion accessory in the rain. Of course they would.

Later managers also suffered personal insults. The Italian Fabio Capello was nicknamed "Postman Pat" and poor old Roy Hodgson was called "Woy" in childish mockery of a slight speech impediment.

Sam Allardyce (who already owned a rather descriptive nickname) lasted only one match. He was caught in a sting – operation by Daily Telegraph reporters posing as businessmen. Sam offered them advice on how to get around the F A rules on 3rd party ownership of players. He was forced into resigning. At least Sam whose England team won 1-0 over Slovakia, can always say that he has a 100% record managing the national side.

Now his successor Gareth Southgate has, so far, done an admirable job, both in choosing a squad, building up team camaraderie and in his dealings with the media. But Gareth (if you're reading this and I know you are) don't for one minute kid yourself that they're not going to come for you.

* * * *

The next poem, is one I penned in 2006, just after England's first foreign manager Sven-Goran Eriksson, announced that he was soon to stand down. Sven had a fairly decent record, but was also found to be rather fond of the ladies. This, of course was lapped up by the tabloids but frowned upon by the powers that were… England Expects!! But the fact that Sven was going all the way with these fair maidens (well, according to the News of the World) while bringing mighty England only to the quarters meant there was going to be just one conclusion.

The media demanded an end to the foreign fertilization of football and called for an Englishman to restore the nation's pride. The names of the usual squeaky wheels were rolled around bars and committee tables. "We want Sam," "Arry's got to get it," "Surely Stuart," were the names most frequently screamed out from Fleet Street.

But the best English manager of that era hardly got a mention. Steve Coppell, who started his managerial career at Crystal Palace, aged just 28, and managed them four times, had just guided unfashionable Reading to the Premiership. Capped 42 times for his country, to this day at Reading and Palace he is referred to as Sir Steve. Maybe if he was appointed England manager, and had a successful 2010 World Cup, "Sir Steve' would have gone from nickname to official title.

For reasons unknown he was never offered the England job, but being the intelligent fella that he is, I'd like to think that if he had, he would have told the suits at Soho Square to place the managerial position in the part of their anatomy that receives the least amount of sunlight.

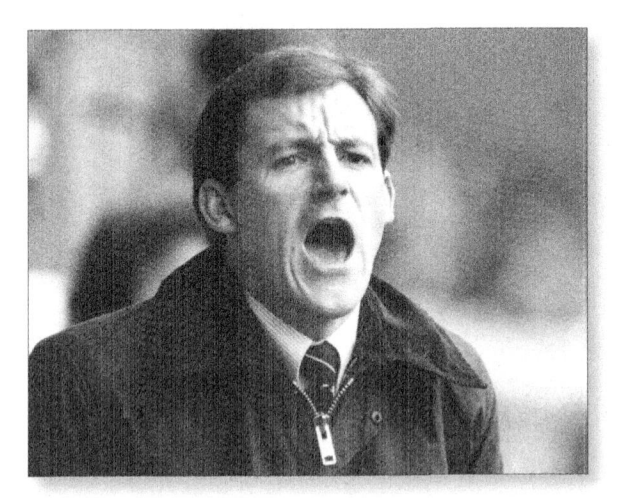

Steve Coppell in 1989. Attribution to Associated Sports Photograph. ASP — Neal Simpson.

ARISE SIR STEVE

"The next manager must be English,
Patriotic, proud and fierce
Someone like Sam Allardyce,
Curbishley or Pearce."

These are the popular sentiments
And everyone's agreed
That it should be a homegrown offering
Who'll take over from the Swede.

The Swede being Sven – Goran Eriksson,
Has been accused of lacking soul

John J. O'Connor

Now when the World Cup's over
He'll be signing on the dole.

So the FA men of Soho Square
Now have the job to choose
Who is the man most qualified
To fill Sven's pumped up shoes.

Over G and T's they'll toss names around
While guessing who Sven might be bedding
Better they should drive up the old M4
To the little town of Reading.

There they'd meet an unassuming man
Who'd just led Reading to promotion
One who's remembered at his former clubs
With fondness and devotion.

A Uni education
And Man United playing career
Steve Coppell managed Palace
Before his thirtieth year
He took the Palace boys to Wembley
Was at the helm during administration
Refused to accept his wages
To help avoid their liquidation.

A successful spell at Brentford
Before heading further west
And he's managed Reading to the Prem
Where they'll battle with the best.

Once Upon a Rhyme in Football

But when you press your remote control
And flick through with your thumb
All you'll see is Allardyce
With his earphones and his gum.
Stuart Pearce with his psycho stare
That could an advancing army topple
But not a mention of the man himself
Reading's Stevie Coppell

So if the FA has the guts
To see if he'll achieve,
Maybe we'll hear
After the next World Cup
Will you please "ARISE SIR STEVE! "

Sorry, I sort of rambled on a bit in that last introduction. We'll now lighten it up some and get away from funerals and people getting the sack. Here's a lighthearted play on team names, nicknames and the names of footballers and managers. This is part one of a three-part series called Football Farm. I hope some of the names bring back memories. Not to worry, I won't bombard you with the three parts all at once.

FOOTBALL FARM (Part One)

Relax now for a Brian Little while,
Get yourselves all nice and calm
And take a trip along with me
Into my football farm.
Malcolm MacDonald owns this old George Farm
Says the sign on the Eric Gates
As we go to meet the footballers
With the animalistic traits.

We'll greet the old John Farmer
On this chilly Mervyn Day

Once Upon a Rhyme in Football

And head into the Tony Field
With the Tim Flowers and David Hay.
As we John Wark along the Rodney Marsh
In the freezing morning fog
We catch a glimpse of Terry Bullock
And ex-United Graeme Hogg.
We don't see Lenny Badger,
He's below ground in a hole
Along with all the miners,
Who dig for Andy Cole.
We see 'The Cat,' Bonetti,
Leaping from a Michael Branch
As we venture even further
Into this football ranch.
The Stags of Mansfield Ian Rush-ing by
With West Ham's Brian Dear
Watching out for Ruel Fox
And Black Cats prowling near.
"Animals !!" Ramsey called the Argies,
Which has to make us laugh
As we spot his number five that day,
Jack Charlton, "the Giraffe"
Then out of one of the Peter Barnes,
Strolls a weary looking ass
It's Tony Adams 'The Donkey"
He of the long-hoofed pass.
"Look!! There's Colin Bell 'Nijinsky,'
The Man City player of course
And Emlyn Hughes of Liverpool,

John J. O'Connor

Known as the 'Crazy Horse.'
Rolling in his pen area, looking rather big
Is keeper Tommy Lawrence,
Liverpool's 'FLYING PIG.'

We see the Rams of Derby,
As to the Mick Hill we get nearer
Playing very defensively,
Afraid of Alan Shearer.
The field is full of rodents,
Just like an unkempt house
And we come across Kev Keegan,
Known as the 'Mighty Mouse.'
They say don't feed the animals,
But we don't really care
As we toss an old Jim Bone
Towards Celtic's 'Yogi Bear.'
We feed 'the Goat,' Shaun Goater
City's Bermudan star
And we hurl bananas at 'Monkey Reid,'
As he swings on a crossbar.
We see Tigers from Hull City,
And Lions from Mill-Wall
Lev Yashin the big 'Black Panther,'
And Wolverhampton's Stevie Bull.
We spot the nasty Norman Hunter,
With his loaded Bryan Gunn
Which he aims at Barry Venison
And kills him just for fun.

Once Upon a Rhyme in Football

"He's killed BARMBY!!!!"
We hear an Eric Young girl cry
As we put a stop to the Roger Hunt
So no one else will die.
It's been a long and tiring day,
The clouds turning Eddie Gray
Now it's time to Ernie Hunt around,
For a place where we can stay.
We eat some Tony Currie,
And get ready for our bed
Which isn't in Notts Forest
But in the farmers Chelsea Shed.
We sample an Alan Knight-cap,
Of Geoff Strong local cider
And we notice a David Webb being spun
By Rachid Harkouk the Palace 'Spider.'
We spend the night in the Eric Black,
Telling scary Peter Storeys
As we hear the Wolves a – howling,
About all their old past glories.
So tomorrow is another day,
When we check out Football Birds
So I have to go to sleep now
To dream up some new words.

There were nine goalkeepers named in that last piece. The next one is also about a goalkeeper; the one and only Pat Jennings. The Premiership now has an abundance of quality goalkeepers. Unfortunately, not too many of them are English.

Back in the day England had no such problem. Gordon Banks was ranked by many as the best in the world. Ray Clemence was amazingly agile, great at coming for crosses, and a lynchpin of that great Liverpool team of the 70's. Then there was Peter Shilton who went on to collect a record 125 caps for England and Phil Parkes of West Ham, who was capped only once but was rated in some circles as possibly the best of the lot.

My own favourite footballer of all time was Crystal Palace's John (Stonewall) Jackson. A man who almost single handedly kept Palace in the Old First Division for four seasons. He was without a doubt the finest un-capped keeper of his generation. Joe Corrigan at Man City, Alex Stepney at Man United and Peter Bonetti at Chelsea also get honorable mentions.

But despite all those great names, one man who in my opinion stood head and hands above them all was Irishman Pat Jennings. He played in four FA Cup finals, the finals of two World Cups, and was capped a record 119 times by Northern Ireland before retiring in 1986. He is one of the few men who could wander down a Highbury back street and be warmly greeted and receive the same acclaim on a stroll down the Tottenham High Road. Also, he is probably the only Catholic in the universe who could ramble along the Loyalist Shankhill Road in Belfast, venture into a few dodgy boozers and not have to put his massive hand into his pocket all night. Here is his story.

Pat Jennings as a teenager in 1964. Attribution ALAMY

BIG PAT FROM THE COUNTY DOWN

This poem's my opinion,
There's no scientific proof
And some readers they will disagree
And say it's not the truth.
It's about the greatest keeper
That I have ever seen
A giant of an Ulster man
With the padded shirt of green.
They talk of Banks and Yashin,
Tomaszewski the Polish clown
But the finest stopper of them all
Hailed from the County Down.
His name was Patrick Jennings,

John J. O'Connor

He was agile, tall and brave
And the sporting headlines of the day,
Of his performances would rave.
He started out at Watford,
Then moved to White Hart Lane
Making his debut in 64
He began his first team reign.
They said his hands were shovels,
But they were more like JCB's
As he plucked the ball out of the air,
One handed with such ease.
He also scored against Man United
In the FA Charity Shield
Beating Alex Stepney with a mighty punt up field.

A laid-back, unassuming man
Who was rarely interviewed,
Even at away grounds
You'd never hear him booed.
After thirteen great years at Tottenham,
He moved just up the road
And Arsenal's Highbury stadium
Became his new abode.
He starred in two World Cups
In Mexico and Spain
Where Northern Ireland's spirit
Won them world acclaim.
He enjoyed great times with Arsenal,
Gathering up more silverware

But his creaking body told him,
'twas time for the rocking chair.

So, the arguments will rage on,
Was the greatest Zoff or Zenga
And you'll hear the name Dave Seaman,
Brought up by Arsene Wenger.
Some will say Sepp Maier,
But they have to be taking the 'Michael'
And of course, Man United fans
Will bring up Peter Schmeichel.
Old timers, they will throw in names,
Frank Swift – Elijah Scott
But I know that Big Pat Jennings
Was the finest of the lot.
The youngsters too will have their views,
And mention Cech and Kahn
But as they say in Ulster,
"Big Patrick, he's yer marn."

Now gather all your evidence
And put it to the jury
And when the verdict is announced
They'll pick the man from Newry.
So put him in the Hall of Fame
And place on his head a crown
For the greatest keeper of them all
**WAS BIG PAT
FROM THE COUNTY DOWN.**

Another great Northern Ireland goalkeeper was Manchester United's Harry Gregg. He played 210 times for the club and represented Northern Ireland in the 1958 World Cup in Sweden, where he was voted the best goalkeeper in the tournament.

Despite his heroics between the sticks, it was because of a terrible tragedy a few months before that World Cup that Harry Gregg will be most remembered.

February 6th, 1958 was the day that British European Airways flight 609, carrying the Manchester United team back from a European Cup tie crashed taking off from the Munich runway. The death toll was 23 passengers including eight United players. One of the two journalists killed was Frank Swift, the ex-Manchester City goalkeeper who was working for the News of the World.

Harry Gregg (r) – centre half Bill Foulkes (l) and Daily Mail photographer Pete Howard. This photo was taken on February, 7th, 1958, the morning after the crash. Attribution ALAMY

Harry Gregg freed himself from the wreckage charged back into the burning plane and started dragging passengers to safety. He was credited with saving many lives that day, including that of his manager Matt Busby, and the great Bobby Charlton. He was also the man who pulled a pregnant Vera Lukic – the wife of a Yugoslav diplomat – to safety along with her two – year – old daughter Vesna. Those were Harry's greatest saves.

HARRY'S GREATEST SAVES

As passengers moaned
And writhed with pain
Some were saved by Harry
From Coleraine.
As injured victims for life did beg
Back into the plane dived Harry Gregg
A Man United and Northern Ireland great
A hero in February of 58
Playing with United less than a year
On that fateful day he showed no fear.
An accomplished keeper
Calm and brave
He could be counted on
To pull a top – shelf save.
But of the many saves
He made as a pro
The best ones of all
Were in the Munich snow.

Unlike the two previous goalkeepers, Ray Clemence never got to play in the World Cup finals. He was a member of the squad that went to Spain in 1982 but was understudy to Peter Shilton. During the 70's Clemence and Shilton competed against each other for the sole ownership of the England number one shirt. For a few years there was so little to choose between them that the manager would play them in alternate games. Eventually Shilton made the position his own but not before Clemence had been capped an impressive 61 times. It always made for a good fans debate: Who was the better of the two? Personally, I thought Clemence, with his superb catching ability on crosses, was slightly better than Shilton.

His ex-Liverpool teammate Graeme Souness was in no doubt about how good Clemence was. After the team he was managing,

Clemence in 1970 – Attribution Sport and General.

Blackburn Rovers, defeated Tottenham in the 2002 League Cup Final, Graeme was asked about the match winning performance from his goal custodian, the American, Brad Friedel. Graeme, not renowned for handing out praise to his players was uncharacteristically gushing with compliments on Brad's performance. However, he ended up the accolades by starting his final sentence with the words, "Don't Get me Wrong."

"DON'T GET ME WRONG"

Graeme Souness, of his keeper
Brad Friedel did rave
As he acknowledged his brilliance
For an exceptional save.
"If it were nae for Brad
Blackburn would have
Got hammered today
It was only himself
That kept Tottenham at bay."
He said, "Brad's better than Bosnich
That bloke from Australia
And more agile than Seaman
And Spain's Pepe Reina.
He reminds me of Shilton
In that he hardly does wrong
No wonder our fans
Sing his name out in song."
With the interview near finished
Graeme thought hard and long

John J. O'Connor

And he started his last sentence
By saying, "Don't get me wrong ...

"DON'T GET ME WRONG,
HE'S NO RAY CLEMENCE."

While we're on the subject of goalkeepers, who remembers that great Mexican World Cup of 1970? Those of us of a certain vintage will recall it as a time when we collected Esso coins that had the faces of the players engraved on them; or sang along to Back Home, England's World Cup anthem, and sneaked downstairs in the early hours of the morning to watch live coverage from exotic-sounding cities like Guadalajara. These had names which our great British commentators put no linguistic effort whatsoever into pronouncing properly. Foreign players became household names and even non-Catholic children would bless themselves down the park when they scored a goal. Just as they'd seen the great Jairzinho of Brazil doing.

As World Cup holders, England had the hopes of the nation on their 1970 shoulders as they headed off to the land of the Aztecs with arguably their best side ever. The full backs of 66, Cohen and Wilson had been replaced by Keith Newton of Everton and Terry Cooper of Leeds. Alan Mullery and Brian Labone had taken the reins from the aging Nobby Stiles and Jack Charlton while up-front Manchester City powerhouse Francis Lee had taken over from Roger Hunt.

A 1-0 defeat by Brazil in a group game did not dampen the spirit of the nation; instead, fans drooled over the save of the century that Gordon Banks made from Pele. So, when England defeated Czechoslovakia to qualify for the quarter finals, press and public alike all agreed that it would be an England v Brazil final. Banksy was practically unbeatable and the West Germans, England's opponents in the quarter finals, were going to get another dose of what they'd got at Wembley in '66.

Unfortunately, Banks might have been able to stop most shots, but he couldn't stop the mishap that resulted in him missing the game. A game in which after 60 minutes England were 2-0 up and cruising.

Then it all started to go wrong. The Germans pulled a goal back through Beckenbaur, and Ramsey with the semi-finals in mind took off Bobby Charlton and replaced him with Colin Bell. The German's tied it up to force extra time and in the 108th minute the great Gerd Muller (der Bomber) scored the winner to give the Jerries a 3-2 victory.

After the game Banksy's replacement Peter Bonetti was, very unfairly I thought, the scourge of the nation. Here's the story with a little bit of that poetic license that we rhymers are supposed to have at our disposal.

Juanito. the Mexican mascot for the 1970 World Cup.
Attribution: Deutshe Presse Agentur (DPA)

WEST GERMANY'S AND MONTEZUMA'S REVENGE

England the reigning champions,
Despite losing to Brazil,
Had reached the quarter finals
And now had time to kill.
Sir Alf Ramsay got the squad together
And gave them all a lecture
"I don't expect you to be choir boys
Or study local architecture.
Have a drink by all means chaps,
But be careful where you go
Avoid the local women and the tainted H-2-0.
Make sure you're back by cur-few
Show some common sense
Tomorrow we're discussing weaknesses
In West Germany's defence.
Keep away from jewelry shops*
And keep out of the sun
Now go out and enjoy yourselves,
Relax and have some fun."

So, the players split into several groups
To see what they could see
One group was led by Alan Ball
And one by Franny Lee.

---

*Before the tournament Bobby Moore was arrested in Colombia and accused of stealing a bracelet in a jewelry shop

John J. O'Connor

But the leader on the pitch
Was the leader off it too
And Bobby Moore led a group
Of just the chosen few.

Along with Banks and Charlton,
Cooper, and Geoff Hurst
Mooro searched the dusty streets
For a place to quench their thirst.
A few mad dogs walked with them
As the sun scorched down at noon
But then Geoff Hurst let out a roar
When he spotted a saloon.

"Welcome to my cantina,"
said the owner looking proud
"Gracias ," said Mooro,
As he surveyed the local crowd.

Mooro bought the bar a drink
And the locals joined their ranks
The main attraction for them being
The modest Gordon Banks.
Banks had been the hero
In the battle with Brazil
And his save from Pele's header
Is shown and talked of still.

"Senor Banks es numero uno,"
agreed the locals to a man

Once Upon a Rhyme in Football

"If Pele cannot beat you,
no way Gerd Muller can."

The owner put some food out,
Large plates of beans and rice
And into Banksy's drink
He slipped some cubes of ice.
A Mariachi band arrived
And played old songs of yore
Of how they drove the Spaniards
Back to their native shore.
The English players politely clapped
At all the local bards
And then sat down among themselves
To play a game of cards.

The drinks they kept on flowing
As Cooper split the deck
But Banksy's glass resembled
The old Titanic wreck.
As Charlton dealt the cards out
For the umpteenth game of rummy
Banksy complained that he was feeling sick
As he pointed to his tummy.
Soon the man who was between the posts
For the '66 World Cup
Had his head in a Mexican toilet bowl
Violently throwing up.

John J. O'Connor

They made it back to their hotel
Just beating Alf's cur – few,
But Gordon never slept that night,
He just stayed awake to spew.
Next day the dreaded sweats came on,
First hot ones then the cold
"It's just a twenty-four-hour bug,"
By the doctor he was told.
They wrapped poor Gordon up with towels
And pumped him full of pills
But next night in his hotel room
He still shivered with the chills.

The day before the German game
He still wasn't near his best
But Alf told him, "Get kitted out"
To take a fitness test.
Alf took a shot at Banksy,
He kicked it soft and lame
And when Gordon caught it easily
Alf said, "Right! you're playing in the game."

Next day the players all gathered
For a pre-match team discussion
But halfway through poor Gordon Banks,
To the toilet he was rushing.
"Put high crosses in on Maier," said Alf,
"It's something that they fear,"
But all that Gordon cared about

Was his fight with diarrhea.
He interrupted Ramsay's speech,
And with his head held down in shame
Announced to all and sundry
That he could not play the game.
Ramsay didn't miss a beat,
His eyelids didn't bat.
Instead, he looked around the room
And pointed to "The Cat."
"You'll start in goal Peter!
Make sure you are prepared."
He said to 'The Cat Bonetti'
Who looked a trifle scared.

So the team they went to Leon
Where the Germans broke their reign
And when the game was over,
They were heading for the plane
Up two-nil and cruising
They took Charlton off for Bell
And the Germans took advantage
Making Bonetti's life a hell.
The Jerries finally won 3-2
To reach the final four
And "Bonetti lost the World Cup"
Would be chanted evermore.

A few days later the Mexican press
Reported some very happy news

John J. O'Connor

Of a local man who won a fortune,
Betting the England team would lose.
He not only forecast their demise
But bet Banksy wouldn't start.
He said it was a premonition
From the Sacred Heart.

In his seedy little cantina
In a run – down part of town
He told the hordes of media
How one night the Lord came down.
He served them up Tequilas
And with them shared the joke
While Gordon Banks was on the loo
Somewhere back in Stoke.

The moral of that poem is
Abroad folks seem so nice
But always keep an eye out
For the man with the cube of ice.

Nowadays, friction between the Germans and the English is confined to English tourists being ticked off when they roll out of bed hungover at noon to find that the Germans have already acquired a bronze tan after commandeering the deckchairs on the Spanish beach about five hours earlier. Also, the Germans don't miss penalties and the English can't score them. England fans hum the Dambusters tune and sing "Two World Wars and one World Cup," at their bemused Saxon cousins; but as one wag pointed out (no it wasn't Coleen) "isn't it lucky the bloody wars never went to penalties?"

Maybe it wasn't lucky though. If the British and Germans had decided the war on a football match imagine the millions of lives that would have been saved. It's well documented that members of the two armies engaged in football matches along the Western Front on Christmas Day in 1914. Generals on both sides disgusted with the fraternization put a stop to it and within days the two sides were back to what they were getting paid for. Slaughtering one another. Here's the story of that day in a poem called 'Bertie Hislop (No Man's Land hero.)

BERTIE HISLOP (NO MAN'S LAND HERO)

He was born in 1899,
Bert Hislop was his name
And from the time he kicked a ball
He was a natural for the game.
From a tiny Yorkshire village
Where the men worked down the pit
His father told him you won't breathe coal

John J. O'Connor

You'll wear a football kit.

Even at his young age
Scouts were on the prowl
Will he play for Sheff United?
Or perhaps become an Owl?
Would he join Manchester City,
Across the old Pennines?
Only thing they knew was,
He'd never work inside the mines.

Then came 1914,
And the war to end all wars
And a generation of young men,
Arrived on Gallic shores.
One day recruiters came to town,
To sign up volunteers
And Bertie Hislop to his age
Added several years.
Lord Kitchener told the volunteers
The war would all be fun
"Over by Christmas time,"
But he didn't say which one.
Despite pleas from his family
And local football side
Bertie headed off to war torn France
Upon a Dover tide.
His home became a muddy trench
All waterlogged and cold

And his only simple pleasure
Was the cigarettes he rolled.
As he stared into the gluey mud
He saw his local pitch at home
Where he left defenders in his wake
As down the wing he'd roam.
They said he'd play for England
Before reaching twenty-one
But Bertie gave his dreams up
To go and fight the Hun.
While artillery fire and charges
Played havoc with the nerves
Bertie dreamt of beating men
With his body swerves.
He dreamt of Yorkshire pudding
And his mother's mushy peas
And how he wished he'd stayed at home
And listened to her pleas.

Soldiers in the trenches during World War One.

John J. O'Connor

Bertie wrote a letter home
On a freezing Christmas Eve
Telling them he'd soon be home
On at least a two-week leave.
He said he'd miss the Christmas cake
The presents and the trifles
But he had to stay and fight the Huns
With his fellow Yorkshire Rifles.

Then dot on midnight came a sound
From a German trench nearby
As 'Silent Night' in German
Filled the Belgium sky.

"All of us are Saxons,
vee only hate zee French,"
Was shouted at the English lines
From the German trench.
"Happy Christmas Fritz"
Came a voice from the English line
and "Happy Christmas Tommy,"
Replied the men from across the Rhine.
On a frosty Christmas morning,
Beneath a clear blue Flemish sky
Bertie and his colleagues
Were not prepared to die.
They dipped into their rations
And soon began to sing
First some Christmas carols,

Once Upon a Rhyme in Football

Then 'God Save the King.'
As the German trench responded
With the carol 'Good King Wenceslas'
A Boche strolled into No Man's Land
Totally defenseless.
He was joined by a couple more,
The schnapps had made them brave
And towards the English trenches
They gave a friendly wave.
So the men of the Yorkshire Rifles
All put down their guns
And climbed over the sandbagged parapet
To greet the friendly Huns.
Hands were shaken, photos swapped,
Cigs given out like candy
And German schnapps was guzzled,
Along with English brandy.
A couple of Highlanders with a ball
Came to join the banter
And soon two goalposts were put down,
Each a tam 'o shanter.
With their comically ugly pork – pie hats,
The Germans did the same
And before you could say Franz Beckanbaur
You had an international game.

Lots were drawn by soldiers,
To see who'd make the side
And Bertie got the right wing spot

John J. O'Connor

Which filled him up with pride.
He terrorized the Germans
Almost from the start
But not with a machine gun
But with his football skill and heart.
The game was never dirty,
They'd both seen too much blood
But not an inch was given,
On the frozen Ypres mud.

The Germans took an early lead
In the morning cold
And Bert removed his trench coat
And up his sleeves he rolled.
The English ventured forward,
With non-stop goal attacks
But they couldn't rattle Germany
And their stoic backs.
Then young Bertie beat two Jerries
With a swivel of his hips
And he fooled the German keeper
With the most delicate of chips.

When half-time came
They swapped 'round ends
With the score-line one to one
And straight away a pumped-up Bertie
Set off on a run.
With a drop of his young shoulders

And his famous body – swerve
He left defenders in his wake
As in the ball he curved.
The Tommies on the side line
Jumped up when he scored
And even the German players
Stood back to applaud.
But those Germans were resilient
Their team refused to fall
And a blonde Aryan head
Soon made the score two all.
"Feed the ball to Hislop,"
came the side line shouts
As the Tommy's soaked up pressure
From the skillful Krauts.
Then Bertie dribbled with the ball
On one of his mazy runs,
Leaving in his muddy wake
A bewildered bunch of Huns.
He dribbled round the goalie,
And popped it in to score
And everyone on No Man's Land
Forgot about the war!
The Germans then pressed forward,
To try and score their third
But the game abruptly ended
When a single shot was heard.
Captain Wainwright removed his pistol,

John J. O'Connor

And fired it in the air
And ordered all the happy Tommy's,
Back into their lair.

Bert returned to the trench
Carried shoulder high
A hero in a brilliant match,
That history would deny.
The history books will tell you
Of hat tricks by Geoff Hurst
But they won't mention Bertie Hislop
Who buried his one first.
They'll acknowledge one man shows,
Malcolm MacDonald's five v Cyprus
But they won't tell of Bertie Hislop
In No Man's Land in Ypres.

Captain Wainwright told the troops,
He sincerely apologized
"I had to stop the game men
Before they equalized.
One thing you'll someday learn chaps,
when you get as old as me
Is you never let the Germans
take you to penal—ties.
You'll beat them out at warfare,
at rugger and at cards
But you'll never beat the bastards
at scoring from twelve yards."

Once Upon a Rhyme in Football

The night before his two week leave,
Bert took up sentry duty
Dreaming of his second goal
Which everyone called a beauty.
He heard a sound in No Man's Land,
And foolishly raised his head
And a seasoned German sniper
Shot Bert Hislop dead.

In a desolate mining village
Which Maggie helped destroy
There lies a grave upon the hill
of a heroic Yorkshire boy.
The stone says BERTRUM HISLOP
15 years 200 days
Killed in action YPRES
And in this ground he lays.
So when you list your English heroes
And put Beckham at the top,
Spare a thought for NO MAN'S LAND
And a lad called BERT HISLOP.

Okay, let's get away from the vomit decorated toilet bowls and dusty streets of Guadalajara – the mud and blood of the World War One trenches and take a trip into the sky with part two of Football Farm called Football Birds.

FOOTBALL FARM (Part Two)
FOOTBALL BIRDS

We wake up nice and early
Have a Barry Fry and wash
And go and check the birds out,
And I certainly don't mean Posh.
As we gaze up at the Sky Blues,
Towards the eastern Sun Jihai
We notice Andy Gray,
Who's working there for SKY.
Because it's a beautiful David MAY day,
The first species that we see

Once Upon a Rhyme in Football

Buzzing along contently, Michael Summerbee.
We see the Bluebirds, and Mark Robbins
Magpies and Palace Eagles
And there is Alan Mullery
With his Brighton Seagulls.
Garrincha, the Brazilian 'songbird'
Dummying all the clouds,
And the Canaries from Carrow Road,
Singing tunes out loud.
John Bird of Cardiff flying by
Watching 'Budgie' Byrne below
And we see that bloke from Villa,
I think his name's Vic Crowe.
Next, we stroll into the old Chris Woods
And survey the Les Green trees
And we spy the Watford Hornets,
Near a swarm of Brentford Bees.
We're being careful of the Andy Thorns,
And the Lee Sharpe – Partick Thistle
When all of a sudden from a tree,
We hear a ref's loud whistle.
It's the man in black Pat Partridge,
Watching the pears grow
And we ask him who his father is,
But he doesn't seem to know.
We hear the Owls of Sheffield,
Giving off a hoot,
And we see Joe Royle and Gerry Queen
On their Gerry Daly shoot.

John J. O'Connor

We come across Mark Parrot,
He repeats all that we say,
And we see the Bradford Bantams,
From City not P.A*
We venture into Tim Sherwood Forest,
The home of Harry Hood
And we nod to Adrian Littlejohn,
Who is chopping Alfie Wood.
He shows us, his David Cross bow,
And his large Mark Bowen arrow
Then aims it at a Paul Birch tree
And shoots down poor John Sparrow.
We retire that night, quite early,
We've had enough we all decide
    Cos tomorrow is a big day
    DOWN by the RIVERSIDE

---

*P.A.- Bradford Park Avenue. They were demoted from the Football league in 1970

As I've said I'm a Crystal Palace fan. There have been times when I wish I wasn't. But whereas you can get rid of wives, quit jobs and find a new local boozer, you can't change team allegiances. Unless of course you are one of those much-travelled modern footballers who, after signing a multi-million-pound contract, swear on their new club badge that they've supported the team since childhood and will continue to support it evermore. Or at least until another team, two places higher in the league comes in with the offer of an extra grand a week. Anyway, the next poem is entitled 'Crystal Palace 1969-79.' It was an eventful ten years for the club, starting with our first ever appearance in the topflight. We gallantly hung on to that berth for four years before, under the guidance of Malcolm Allison

Crystal Palace players celebrate after beating Fulham and winning promotion to the Old First Division in 1969. Attribution – Press Association / Hamsworth.

we suffered back-to-back relegations. A trip in the 75-76 season – to the semi-finals of the F.A Cup helped ease the pain. Eventually after three seasons spent in the Third division and two in the Second, we eventually clawed ourselves back up to the top division.

We did it on a Friday night in May of 79 (the night before the Cup Final) when in front of a record crowd of 51,801 we defeated Burnley 2-0 to win promotion and go up as champions. Despite this piece being about Palace I'm sure many football fans who were following their team and giving it large in that era will identify with many parts of it.

CRYSTAL PALACE MEMORIES 1969–79

Bobby Woodruff, Mark Lazarus,
David Payne in the Roger Hynd
3-2 against Fulham in 1969.
Players giving shirts away
Fans all on the pitch.
Finding out that in the First Division
Life can be a bitch.
First game v Man United
Two-all and a record crowd
Selhurst Park had never,
Ever been that loud.
Skinheads and hippies
Shrunken Levi jeans
Ben Sherman shirts and braces
Worn by brooding teens.

Once Upon a Rhyme in Football

Kember going to Chelsea,
He was the local boy
Alan Birchenall, Tony Taylor,
John Jackson, Roger Hoy.
Tank tops, hats, and cardigans,
In the colours of the team
Anglo Italian Cup,
And each year the Wembley dream.
"Queen in brawl at the Palace"
Was a famous headline shown.
But it was about our Gerry Queen
Not old Lizzie on the throne.
Ted Heath, Thornton Heath,
Northwood Road, Addington Rule
Late goal v Leeds United
By John 'the Shovel' Sewell.

Signing players whose time had passed
Who were doing their final rambling
Charlie Cooke and Yogi,
Willie Wallace, Scott and Tambling.
Peanuts for Sixpence,
Knees up Muvver Brown
Every year the experts saying
That we were going down.

Taking swimming lessons,
Before Nott'm Forest away —[*]

---

[*] For a period in the 1970's, Nottingham Forest supporters had a nasty habit of hurling rival supporters into the River Trent.

John J. O'Connor

The Trent could be quite nasty,
On a cold December day.
Reject players to Orient,
T.Rex, Slade and Sweet.
Playing all the London teams,
And always getting beat.

Yogi's pair v Sheffield, a super 5-1 win
On Match of the Day that evening
So we all had to stay in.
De De De De Don Rogers,
Stuart Jump the Peter Wall
And John Jackson for England,
Was the pleading Holmesdale call.
5-0 v Man United, sure it's written in folklore
If it wasn't for Alex Stepney,
We could have scored four more.

Doctor Martens sprayed with silver,
Some were sprayed with gold
And Parka anoraks, to fight the winter cold.
Palace Dollies, Glad all Over,
Old ma Minchella selling peanuts
And police brutality taking place,
Inside the Holmesdale police huts.
"As I see it BERT HEAD MUST GO"
read the banner every game
And Palace's board of directors
Seemed to think the same.

Big Mal's arrival at the Palace
Greeted with elation
Defeat at Carrow Road assigned us relegation.
Two tone tonic pants
And loafer shoes well shone
Things were going to change
Under Malcolm Allison.
The Claret and Blue, becoming Red and Blue,
The Glaziers are the Eagles
Big Mal chomping Cubans,
No time for Embassy regals.

Mal being Mal, at the Playboy club, Mayfair, London 1973. Attribution – Press Association

John J. O'Connor

Nodding discreetly to fellow fans
When you saw them at Millwall.
Jackson leaving Palace,
With his head held tall.
Peter Taylor beating defenders
As down each wing he'd burst
Paddy Mulligan, Jeffrey Johnson
And David Swindlehurst.
Timpson coaches from East Croydon,
The Railway Travelers Club,
Watney's Party Sevens,
And motorway cafe grub.
Relegation to Division Three,
After a night of tears in Wales,
Bobby Kellard and Roy Barry,
Both as tough as nails.
Tooting and Mitcham away,
On a Wednesday afternoon
The dregs of society show,
Inflicting many wounds.
Away day trips to Brighton,
To Port Vale and Halifax
Jeffries and Jim Cannon solid at the back.
Defeat at Plymouth in the Cup,
With Venables missing a pen
Praying to have a wedding
When we're playing at the Den.
Terrace surges, New Stand singing,
Thousands going away

Once Upon a Rhyme in Football

But in the old Third Division
For three years we have to stay.
Champagne, cigars, fedoras,
Drawing attention to the club
And the day Fiona Richmond
Ended up in the players' tub.
David Kemp and Phil Holder,
Nick Chatterton the groundman's son.
1976— when the Cup was nearly won.
Swindles goal at Leeds, Chelsea on the pitch[*]
Whittles goal at Roker,

Celebrating the victory at Sunderland in the Cup quarter finals at Roker Park in 1976. Attribution Harmsworth photo library.

---

[*] Chelsea on the pitch. Known as the Valentine's Day Massacre. Crystal Palace went to Stamford Bridge on February 14th, 1976, and knocked Chelsea out of the F.A Cup. Trouble broke out between rival fans and police horses were brought onto the terraces to restore order. Many fans ended up on the side of the pitch.

John J. O'Connor

And the semi at the Bridge.
Taylor capped for England,
Whilst playing in the Third
And an average 20,000
Making sure they're heard.

Birmingham bags and flares,
That we've conveniently forgotten
Stranglers and the Clash,
The Jam and Johnny Rotten.
Kenny Sansom's debut,
At Tranmere on a Tuesday night
Big Mal resigning, and to Turkey taking flight.
Venables being appointed,
Paul Hammond, Tony Burns
Rachid 'Spider' Harkouk,
Fooling defenders with his turns.
A 1-0 win v Brighton
At a rainy Chelsea ground
Mullery throwing change around
And acting like a clown.

Trips to the North of England,
And greetings at the station.
"Have you got the time mate?"
It could be a dodgy situation.
Hy Money taking photos,
Len Chatterton mowing the lawn
Martin Hinshelwood, Billy Gilbert,

Once Upon a Rhyme in Football

Ian Walsh and Jeffrey Bourne.
Winning big at Wrexham
And pipping them to the post
Opening bottles of champers
As we gave the team a toast.

Perms coming into fashion,
Mustaches no longer cool
And Doris* scoring a cracker,
In the Cup v Liverpool.
The sound of Evans' leg being shattered,
By Fulham's Georgie Best
Starting to play the youngsters,
Who were ready for the test.
Jerry Murphy, Terry Fenwick,
Vince Hilaire, and Peter Nick
And the return of Stevie Kember
To help the midfield click.
Playing super football,
John Burridge in the goal
Maggie in power, and thousands on the dole.
Sideburns** selling programmes,
Wings and Mull of Kintyre
And the EAGLES from South London,
Soaring higher and higher.

---

* Doris- Paul Hinshelwood, Palace full back who was affectionately referred to as Doris, due to the perm hair style he wore.
** Sideburns. Crystal Palace's legendary programme seller. Also called Sido.

John J. O'Connor

1979, on Friday May 11
Palace fans are thinking,
They have finally got to heaven.
2-0 v relegated Burnley,
Who we had always on the run
And the promotion party witnessed
By fifty-one thousand, eight hundred and one.
Celebrations on the pitch,
The Holmesdale in full song
And Crystal Palace returning
RIGHT BACK WHERE WE BELONG

One thing is for sure, they'll never squeeze over 51,000 into Selhurst Park again, just as they won't see crowds of over 79,000 at Goodison or 135,000 at Hampden Park. After disasters like Ibrox and Heysel the days of the football terrace were numbered. Hillsborough, where 96 Liverpool fans lost their lives, was the final straw and football has pretty much reverted to all-seater stadiums.

Like most fans my age I miss the old terrace. I really believe that someone in authority should show a bit of common sense and allow safe standing areas in each stadium. Let's face it, at most grounds now there are sections where the fans stand up throughout the game anyway. This isn't always fair on the elderly and the fans who just want to sit down to have a quiet afternoon snooze or dip into the creative organic sarnies their partner has carefully prepared for them.

A young fan being passed down to the front at Chelsea v Arsenal in 1947
Attribution: Alamy

Realistically the terrace, like the television repairman or the rag-and-bone man is a relic of the 20th century. The memory lives on though in the pictures and film reels of terraces packed tightly with a mass of working-class humanity. Terraces, where kids were passed down to the front by older fans with prematurely aged faces. Faces that had witnessed poverty and wars and where for a few hours on a Saturday they were free from the worries of the working man's life. It was a place where fans stood on tiptoe for a view. It was also a place where they surged, swayed, swore, prayed, moaned, groaned, fought, sang, and cried as they urged their team on. So they took away our terraces, but they could never take the memories.

GOOD-BYE TO THE TERRACE

The terrace has gone
It no longer could last
Modernization made it
A thing of the past.
No more youngsters being passed
To the front for a view
Or fans jammed together like paper to glue.

Sometimes the scene,
Of thrown bottles and rocks
The terrace was banished
Like the mines and the docks.
Fans came to realize,
To pro-gress we must change
But the atmosphere's gone now

Grounds sound very strange.
Villa Park is a library,
Chelsea's Shed's yuppified
United have the prawn brigade
On board for the ride.
But it's nice to sit down,
Have a half decent view
And not get your back leg warmed
While it's being used as a loo.

So goodbye to the Terrace,
You served fans so well
But you're now part of folklore
Just like William Tell.

John J. O'Connor

One thing about the fans on the terraces — they always had a player who they identified as the King. He wasn't necessarily the team's best player, but the fans would take to him and, usually to the tune of the Christmas carol Noelle, would sing that the said player was the king of whichever ground they played at. Gilzean was the King of White Hart Lane, Colin Bell the King at Man City, Jeff Astle at West Brom, Law at United and of course the great Peter Osgood at Chelsea. Ossie passed away prematurely a few years ago but is still remembered at Chelsea as the King of Stamford Bridge.

KINGS ROAD KING

He always wOS GOOD,
He wos King of the Shed,
He was 60's Kings Road
He filled defenders with dread.
He was a cup winner in 70
He scored in each round
as the Blues beat the Leeds
at the Old Trafford ground.

He played alongside Bonetti,
Hudson and Hutch
He would have won more than four caps
Had he'd been born Dutch.
He was full of great touches,
giving defenders no peace
He won a European medal
On a hot night in Greece

He left the Blues disillusioned,
Headed away for a spell
Played in Philadelphia,
And for the Saints at the Dell.

He won the Cup with Southampton
When Stokes scored one late
And the fans said he Wos Good
But now Ossie Wos Great.
But West London kept calling
Where he was still called 'The King'
And Os returned home for one final fling.
    He wos flamboyant
    He wos skillful
    He could give and take kicks
    R.I.P PETER OSGOOD
    Who ruled S.W.6

Unfortunately, like Ossie, a surprisingly large number of footballers are taken from us at a relatively young age. The late 50s seems to be an especially dangerous age for the once finely tuned athlete. Apparently, it's said, the old ticker expands in the playing days because of supreme fitness, but after retirement it still needs constant activity to keep it in tip-top health.

A player who had a great innings is celebrated now; the great Preston Plumber himself, Tommy Finney, who passed away in 2014 at the age of 91. Football fans have always liked a good argument over which were the better of equally skilled players. At the moment the big debate is who is superior, Ronaldo or Messi? We've had the Lampard – Gerrard debates, Fowler v Owen and Clemence v Shilton. But back in the 1950s it was a toss-up between Finney and Stanley Matthews for the title of the greatest winger on earth. Fans were equally divided.

Finney was a bloke who would definitely put the modern pampered pro to shame. If ever there was a one-man team it was the Preston North End team of the 50's. The press used to dub them "The plumber and his ten drips," and the great Billy Shankly, once a teammate of Finney's said of him, "He must get a great tax rebate because he has ten dependents."

The season after Finney retired, 1960-61, Preston were relegated from the Old First Division. They have never returned. Here is the story of Sir Tommy Finney.

THE PROUD PRESTON PLUMBER

"Excuse us Mr. Finney.
We know later, you have a game
But the outside toilet got blocked last night
And there's a problem with the drain."

"I'll make my way right over,"
said the great man from North End
"I'll just stop by the supply shop
to buy a copper bend."

See, while our modern players
Are being fed pasta and health drinks
Pre – match for Tommy Finney
Was fixing peoples sinks.
He'd then jump on the local bus
He could not afford the rail
And make the journey with the fans
To Preston's ground, Deep – dale.

Tom Finney was born in 22,
A Preston man by birth,
Rated by many in the 50's
As the best wingman on earth.
He made his Preston debut,
At the late age of Twenty-Four
His career having been put on hold,
Until the ending of the war.
The great Bill Shankly said
His own claim to fame
Was sending Finney his first pass
"A right bad un too," quipped Finney
"It went four feet off the grass."

A natural left – footed player,
But who was comfy on both flanks

John J. O'Connor

"He could have played brilliant
with an overcoat"
Was another quote from Shanks.

He'd beat defenders down the line,
With shoulder dips and weaves
And his thirty goals for England
Were the most till Jimmy Greaves.
He won no major trophies,
Though was acclaimed by all his peers
And in '54 and '57,
He won player of those years.
He retired in 1960, to much fanfare and hype
And returned full time, to what he knew,
Bending copper pipe.

*The Preston Plumber – Tom Finney Attribution –
Provincial Press Agency*

Once Upon a Rhyme in Football

He was made a Sir in 98
And a Stand was built in his name
And when they had the opening,
Fans in their thousands came.
They cheered Sir Tommy Finney,
And sang his name aloud
The man who more than anyone
Made Preston North End Proud.
So when you see a Premier player
Pull up pre-match in a Hummer
Remember that he couldn't lace the boots
    Of the bus-riding
PRESTON PLUMBER.

As we all know, Tom Finney's team-mate, the great Bill Shankly went on to build the brilliant Liverpool side of the 60's and 70's. He retired in 1974 and handed over the reins to his sidekick Bob Paisley. Paisley later retired and the job became that of Joey Fagin, another member of the backroom staff. All three of those greats along with Ronnie Moran were part of what became known in football folklore as the Anfield Boot Room. Apparently the four of them were so passionate about the game that after training each day they'd head downstairs, stick on the old kettle and spend hours talking football and discussing tactics. These great men are, like a lot of the managers of that era, no longer with us, but you can bet your life they have found a boot room up above.

THE BOOT ROOM UP IN HEAVEN

Saint Pete went up to God's room,
And told Him there's a prob
"All our football managers
Are in bad need of a job.
They get restless every Saturday,
Especially coming up to three
And some pace up and down the clouds
Looking very jittery.
Down on earth they start a war
When active men are bored
But that's not the way – we do it here"
said Peter to the Lord.

Once Upon a Rhyme in Football

God listened sympathetically,
And swore to lift their gloom
And said to Peter,
"Here's the keys,
let 'em use the 'Old Boot Room.'
They can sit and talk of tactics,
In which on earth they did excel
And let them conjure up a squad,
And I'll arrange a game with Hell."

So, Saint Peter told the managers
Of the room supplied by God
And asked them to work in unison
And try and build a squad.
"I believe they called you gaffers,
in your past lives down below
and you liked to moan at referees
and at each other have a go.
Now remember you're in Heaven,
Where all are kind and caring
So when you're in the Boot Room, lads,
Be careful with the swearing."

The managers they all agreed,
Their excitement showing through
As they sat down to talk of football,
A subject they all knew.

Cloughie sat with Taylor,
A friendship now renewed

John J. O'Connor

And Sir Alf Ramsay sat all alone,
Though he wasn't being rude.
Sir Matt he sat with Mercer,
Two great men of Manc's
And across from them the originals,
Fagin, Paisley, Shanks.

Bill Nicholson spoke with Bertie Mee
Of past great games they'd seen
While Don Revie and Stan Cullis,
Swapped tales with old Jock Stein.
Herbert Chapman from the Thirties,
Spun yarns that made one smile
While Harry Catterick reminisced,
With Ron Greenwood and John Lyall
Bert Head of Palace and Jim Bloomfield
Had a laugh and shared a joke
And also there, in his own armchair,
Was Tony Waddington of Stoke.

The small talk it finally ended
When Cloughie took the floor
As he reminded all the managers,
What they were in the Boot Room for.
"We come from many places men,
And from different eras were our birth
But the thing we have in common is,
We coached football down on earth.
So let's put our football brains together

Once Upon a Rhyme in Football

Swap ideas and have debate
And choose a top-notch squad of players
From those who've walked
Through Heaven's gate."

It was the goal keeping position
That caused the first managerial rift
When Jock Stein said Ronnie Simpson,
And Herb Chapman wanted Swift.
They settled on John Thompson,
Famed in song and prose,
Who died in a Glasgow derby,
Diving at a forwards toes.

Bill Nick chose two ex – Tottenham
John White — to strike the goals
And here's a NICE ONE for you,
For full back CYRIL Knowles.
They all agreed on Dixie Dean,
Wilf Mannion and Sir Stan,
But then the room went silent
As Sir Matt Busby raised his hand.
They listened to his every word,
Like pupils to a master
As he told them of that awful day,
The Munich Air disaster.

"There are eight young players
who've been up here, since 1958
And they're the ones that for this squad,

John J. O'Connor

I'd like to nominate.
Sorry that I'm crying,
But it's still a mournful feeling
As I think of David Pegg,
Geoff Bent and Liam Whelan.
Duncan Edwards, Eddie Colman,
Roger Byrne and young Mark Jones
I can still see all the wreckage
And all the broken bones."

The room went quiet briefly,
But then it lightened up
When Cloughie said they'd have a break
And get a little sup.
They downed some Mild and Bitter,
Then discussions did resume
And they all agreed that life up there,
Was magic in that room.

In between the banter,
And the rehashing of old jokes
Ted Bates of Southampton raised his hand
And named young Bobby Stokes.
"He was a Saint, down below,
now he's one up here as well'
His spirit will forever live,
In our old ground at The Dell."

"Raich Carter is my man," said Clough
"I saw him bury three past Bolton

And for a no-nonsense centre half,
Who else but Big Jim Holton?"
The great George Best on the wing
The new kid on the block
And Colin Bell in midfield
with Baxter and Murdoch."

Pete Osgood and 'Wor Jackie'
In some quarters got a nod
And unanimously they all agreed
To put Davie Cooper in the squad.
Tom Finney and 'Jinky Johnstone'
Are also mentioned for the wing
And even up in Heaven
JEFF ASTLE was 'The King.'
The arguments really started though
About who on the field would guide
Who'd lead the team to victory
Who would captain this great side.
"John Charles" said one, "it has to be
No one led like the GENTLE GIANT"
And the other gaffers with their picks
Were equally defiant.
Busby called for Duncan Edwards
"He was a boy of power and might"
But Stan Cullis butted in
And called for Billy Wright.

Saint Peter popped his head in, and said,
"Lads careful with the din

and remember that, to swear up here
puts you all in the sin – bin."

Don Revie stroked his chin in thought
Then said, "I think I've got a winner
even though some of you might think,
on earth he was a sinner.
I vote for Billy Bremner,
he was superb for me at Leeds.
He was skillful, tough and fiery,
just what this team needs."

"Nay – I've a man to lead," growled Shanks
"Like me he hates to lose,
He's only been up here a while
his name is Emlyn Hughes.
He's been galloping through the clouds
I'll try and rein him in.
This team needs his enthusiasm
and his moral-boosting grin."

Sir Alf Ramsey raised his eyebrows
said sarcastically, "Are you sure?
The only captain for this team,
goes by the name of Robert MOORE.
Bobby was a diamond, in Mexico my jewel
He lifted the World Cup in '66
and was the epitome of cool."

They all looked around and nodded
And agreed he was the man

So the Captain of the Heaven squad
Was MOORO of West Ham.

**THEY NEVER DID GET
THEIR GAME WITH HELL.**

But it didn't cause no gloom
For every day the coaches met
To talk football in that room.
Sometimes they got excited,
And the discussions could get loud
But God was very happy,
It kept them off the corner cloud.

So, as we listen to predictors
Forecasting doom and gloom
The boys upstairs are having a ball
IN HEAVENS OLD BOOT ROOM.

One thing those great managers knew about was how to lead men and how to organize the tactical side of the game. In today's football jargon it would be said that "they knew how to set their stalls out and had man-management skills." Unfortunately, in World War One, millions of lives were lost because the Generals didn't have a clue how to set their stalls out. Lions led by donkeys was a famous saying of the time. The British leadership was still deploying tactics used 70 years previously during the Crimean War. It would be similar to the England team today trying to use the same tactics as Alf Ramsey's wingless wonders did back in 66. …. Oooops! Maybe that wasn't a very good comparison.

Anyway, here comes a poem called Tactical Error that portrays that awful day on July, 1st 1916, when more than 20,000 working class men were wiped out on The Somme by breakfast time. If it had been football managers making the military decisions they'd have been sacked in the morning. Instead, the good old British Army awarded their tactically inept muppets with promotions and medals.

TACTICAL ERROR

July the first, Nineteen Sixteen,
A day of death and terror
A generation lost by brekky
'Cos tacticians made an error.
Pep talk from the Captain
Who's from the playing fields of Eton
He drills into his anxious players
That they never will be beaten.
"Chaps — don't worry about their Arsenal

Just stick to our formation,
And once we have them beaten
We'll have a celebration."
A brandy ration is distributed
To counter pre-match tension
As the players line up to go on the pitch
Full of apprehension.
Some are praying quietly,
Others struggle with their kit
Some can't wait for action
They're chomping at the bit.
ATTACK – ATTACK – ATTACK
Is the tactic of the day
Which seems a little odd
As the lads are playing away.
They're frightened and bewildered
When they hear the whistle blow
As up the ladder and on the pitch
They know they have to go.
Once out on the ripped-up field
They meet a cauldron of sound
But unfortunately for these young lads
This is not a football ground.
This isn't Windsor Park,
or the Hawthorns at West Brom
It's the final game they'll ever play
On a green field called THE SOMME.

To follow on the subject of the Somme....

During the 2018 World Cup in France the 102nd anniversary of the beginning of that battle was commemorated. It put into perspective the reality of how trivial football really is. Meanwhile football Commentators were describing penalty takers as having to face the most stressful scenario human beings could face in their lives. Come on now, give me a break! I'd sooner stroll up and take my chances against a German goal proprietor from twelve yards than charge across No Man's Land while a German machine gun operator, with a bottle of Schnapps and six days' supply of ammunition stacked next to him, used me as target practice. If the numbers of dead were any indication, the Germans were as good with the machine gun as they are taking penalties. The bastards just don't miss.

I mean, unless you're unfortunate enough to be Colombian, what is the worst thing that can happen to a player if he misses a penalty? If you're English, the nation will embrace you. They'll cry with you and a few weeks later you will have your own lucrative television commercial advertising Kleenex or an anti-dandruff shampoo. Of course, six months later when the great British press finds out you were shagging the next door neigbour's wife, you will be ostracized – and your missed penalty will be brought up at every opportunity.

So, we should try and remember that no matter how much footballers sacrifice to get to the top, they never sacrifice a fraction of what those braves souls did when they went over the top.

Once Upon a Rhyme in Football

THE YEAR '16

"Can you imagine how nervous
Lagos Aspas must feel?"
Cried the commentator.
"It must be impossible to feel more nervous.
If he misses, they're out."

"Look how nervous those Argentinian fans are!"
Cried the commentator.
"They have the fear and dread of defeat
Written all over their painted faces.
This fear is real."

"Harrrrrry Kayyyane — what an athlete."
Cried the commentator,
As the ball ricocheted off Kane's foot.
"Has to be up there

The commentator might have got that last announcement wrong.

With the most heroic Englishmen of all time.
"What a joyous place France must be tonight!"
Cried the commentator. . . .
"Then again it was always a joyous place."

For hundreds of thousands of tortured souls
France, until their deaths,
Was always a nightmare.
On this day one hundred and two years ago
Many thousands of men
Were more heroic than Kane
And more nervous than Lagos Aspas of Spain,
More fearful than some fan
Crying for the camera
Thinking his world has ended
Cos his team lost on pens.
Not for the heroes
A commentator complimenting
Their expert shot on the German nests
Or Var recording them
Beating the trap of the wire
Or their dives to the ground
In that cauldron of sound.
"He rolled over like he was dead!"
Cried the commentator.
If he'd been covering the Somme
He'd have been right.

When parents sent their sons off to join the armed forces they mostly hoped, we can presume, that it would discipline them and make men of them. In most cases I don't think they intended their kids to become cannon fodder

Along with "Get yer bloody 'air cut," another phrase often hurled by elders at kids of my generation was, "A few years in the army, that'll put manners on ya!" Well, I doubt very much that anyone ever ordered Wayne Rooney to get his hair cut, but I'm sure a few people thought that a little time in Her Majesty's Armed Forces might have put some manners on the young scally.

It's hard to believe that Wayne Rooney is now 36. As a football fan I'm always going to remember him as that brilliant 16-year-old who scored that terrific goal for Everton against Arsenal. Also, who can forget the brilliant bicycle kick he scored for Manchester United in a match against rivals City in 2011. He was arguably one of the greatest players that England has ever produced. His record 53 goals in 120 appearances for his country is a testament to his greatness.

Another thing that can't be forgotten though is the amount of people forever offering excuses for him when he'd get himself into trouble on and off the pitch. Yes, like a lot of gifted humans, our Wayne could be a bit of a lad at times One of those constantly sticking up for him was his old boss at Old Trafford, Sir Alex Ferguson. Throughout Rooney's nineteenth year, when he seemed constantly in the headlines for the wrong reasons, Fergie would defend him in interview after interview by saying "Och, the wee lad is only nineteen."

Many self-appointed experts put their two-pennies-worth into how to tame Wayne, but the next poem (which is pure fiction) describes what might well have worked to get the early-days Wayne to behave like a respectable member of footballing society.

John J. O'Connor

THE TAMING OF WAYNE ROONEY (HE'S ONLY NINETEEN, YE KNOW)

"A course in anger management?
Remember the boy's just turned nineteen.
We've got to make allowances,
Cos he one of the greatest ever seen."
Others recalled Gazza's,
Psychopathic need to win
But at least the unruly Gazza,
Played football with a grin.

Sir Alex listened to all the advice,
Even the offer of a shrink
Then headed home from Old Trafford,
To have a little think.
He wandered down to his garden shed,
Which was full of books and spanners
And started trying to figure out
How to teach young Rooney manners.
His eyes then caught a dusty book
Which to his face did bring a smile
And he copied numbers out of it
And started them to dial.
He spoke to old ex-footballers
Some short of a bob
Said that he'd look after them
If they'd do him a wee job.
He told the lads he wanted them,

Once Upon a Rhyme in Football

To play his first team in a match
Then went on to explain to them
The plan that he had hatched.
He filled in trustees in the Man U team
All about the plan
And along with the ex-professionals
All were for it – to a man.

The match was on the practice pitch,
With no supporting crowd
A willing ex-ref was hired
And no media allowed.
The ex-pros were bald and graying
Some were overweight
And their mission was to dish out manners
Before it was too late.

They stood out on the frozen pitch
Waited for Man U to appear
Then Giles went straight to Rooney
And whispered in his ear.
Rooney told him to F- Off
And he gave the yap-yap sign
And Nobby Stiles said,
"Leave it John, this little kid is mine."
First time Rooney got the ball,
He eased it past Ron Harris
Then brought it back and beat Ron again
In an effort to embarrass.
He tried it then a third time,

John J. O'Connor

But this time he came a cropper
As he felt a boot land in his groin
Courtesy of Chopper.
"For F's sake Ref!" squeaked Rooney,
Who then screamed a bunch of F's
But along with his dodgy eyesight
Jack Taylor had gone deaf.
Pat Crerand dragged Wayne to his feet
And growled, "How dare ye dive.
If you pull that stunt again lad
ye will nae leave this pitch alive."
Now Rooney's face was grimacing,
Wearing its usual moody scowl
And he went over the top on Storey
With a truly brutal foul.
Dave Mackay came storming over
To lift Rooney by the shirt
And warned the cocky Scouser,
"You're on the way to getting hurt."

But the United players fed Rooney
To let him show off all his skills
And he flew past Norman Whiteside,
And the aging Micky Mills.
Then he pushed the ball past Yorath,
And for goal did start to race
When he was hammered into yesterday
By the fearsome Jimmy Case.
Tommy Smith knelt down to tend him

And have a soothing little word
As he slapped Wayne to attention
To make sure that he was heard.
"I'm a fellow Scouser son,
I've had my share of knocks
I grew up on the Scotland Road,
and me dad worked on the docks.
I never had your talent,
But I always had respect
And if you go by me one more time today,
I'll make sure that you are decked."
Half-time came, and Wayne told Alex
He felt he'd had enough
But Sir Alex laughed right into his face, saying,
"I thought that you were tough."

The second half soon began,
With the ex-pros down by six
And Rooney started to turn it on
With a few old party tricks.
He tried some fancy dummies
And a couple of nutmegs
Then unfortunately he encountered NORMAN,
The one who "Bites Yer Legs."

He yelled at referee Taylor
To give Hunter a red card
But Norman stood and laughed at him
And said, "they told me you was hard!"

John J. O'Connor

As Rooney rubbed his swollen knee
And grimaced with the pain
Hunter and Taylor spoke of kids
And the merits of the cane.
They laughed as Rooney hobbled
And muttered words ending in K
And agreed he was an example
Of inner-town decay.
He screamed abuse at Taylor,
Implying the butcher must be blind
Then got a clip across the ear
From The Girder, Roger Hynd.

They hammered Wayne so much that half,
He started playing as a back
But defending a high corner,
He got clobbered by Big Jack.
"Get in me way again young bairn,
I'll give you a right hook!
And if you annoy me any further,
I'll put your name in my black book."*

Wayne gestured to be taken off
But Fergie pretended he hadn't seen
As Wayne wished he was off the pitch
In his mansion with Coleen.
Then Georgie Best got the ball

---

*Jack Charlton revealed on a 1970 talk show that he had a little black book that contained the names of players who he intended to harm.

Once Upon a Rhyme in Football

And went on an up-field run
Stopped it at Wayne Rooney and gestured,
'Come on son'.
The son of Pool came storming in,
But George threw him a crafty dummy
And as with Gazza, tears rolled down
As Wayne cried for his mummy.

This was a defining moment
Of character transformation
And out there on the pitch began
The Wayne Rooney reformation.
He started calling players Sir
Though they tried to break his bones
And he apologized profusely
After being stomped by Joey Jones.

The whistle went to end the match
United won ten-nil
But the day of Rooney's lesson wasn't over still.
As he shook the hands of the players
Who were walking off the park
He was pulled away towards the ref
By "Sniffer" Alan Clarke.
"Apologize to Jack Taylor, for being such a prat!
and tell him it's the very last time,
you'll ever act like that."

So Wayne said, "Sorry Mister Taylor,
For clapping in your face

John J. O'Connor

I know that to United,
I've been a huge disgrace."
"Seems you've learned your lesson son,
now you're acting like a man.
So concentrate on football,
and be the greatest that you can."

The old Pro's took Rooney out that night,
And fed him real ale made from hops
Told him, "No more Red Bull
Or girlie alcho-pops."
They taught him how to show respect,
Though Georgie Best kept quiet
How to have a good time out,
Without it being a riot.

Next morning at Old Trafford,
Wayne appeared for training early
A happy look upon his face,
Instead of being surly.
"Good morning, Mister Ferguson,"
He said to the Scot's surprise
And he said it most full heartedly,
With a glint in both his eyes.
A pressman asked for an interview
And got a yes instead of no
And Sir Alex looked on proudly saying
"HE'S ONLY NINETEEN YEARS YE KNOW."

The late Norman Hunter, who appeared in that last piece, was a player well capable of putting manners on anyone. The first time I ever saw the phrase "Norman Bites Yer Legs" it was daubed on a banner at the 1972 FA Cup final between Leeds and Arsenal. I often wondered who coined the phrase.

That great Leeds team of the late 60's and 70's was blessed with skilled piano players, but Revie knew that to make it gel and give it balance he also needed a few piano shifters. Norman, like Nobby Stiles at Manchester United, would have been classed as a shifter. Geoff Hurst aside, would England have won the World Cup without Nobby Stiles? Probably not. Would Leeds have won as many trophies without Norman? Absolutely NOT.

Both Norman and Nobby were players whose undoubted footballing ability was often overshadowed by their reputations for being fearsome tacklers who were occasionally a second or ten late with a challenge. But as the next poem shows, the crew upstairs in heaven were well prepared for the arrival of Norman.

*Outside Elland Road, on the day Norman's death was announced.
Attribution: ALAMY*

John J. O'Connor

THEY'RE WEARING CRICKET PADS UP IN HEAVEN

"Why are you putting on cricket pads?"
 Says God to old Saint Pete.
"Cos Norman Hunter just arrived
 and he's dangerous with his feet.
We've put him on Cloud number Six
 where he can hang his England Caps on pegs
 and the cloud is already labeled as
'Norman Bites Yer legs.'
Despite his reputation God," says Pete
"he's liked by all the lads
 but I strongly recommend to you
 that you put on your cricket pads."

Another player who could handle himself was journeyman Bobby Kellard. Not as well-known as many of the so-called hard men, Bobby had an eventful career playing for eight different teams. He had two spells with Palace and two also with Portsmouth. I still remember the captain's performance he put in against Arsenal in April of 1972. Palace were fighting for survival and every point counted. The Gunners took a 2-0 lead but then Bobby took the game by the scruff of the neck and almost single-handedly dragged Palace back into the game with his dogged determination. The match ended up 2-2 and is remembered, by all Palace fans who were present, as the Bobby Kellard game. Bobby liked the odd barney and he entered the history books by being the first English professional footballer sent for an early Sunday bath, when he was playing for Pompey against Orient in an FA Cup replay in January of '74. The title of the poem sums him up.

Bobby Kellard (r) in action for Crystal Palace against Leicester's Alan Birchenall. Attribution – Fotosports International.

John J. O'Connor

BOBBY KELLARD
(HE WAS WELL 'ARD)

Some players are born to ramble
Others play for just one side
Bobby Kellard played for eight different teams
And led them all with pride.
Robert Sydney William Kellard
A north Londoner by birth
A born and natural, feisty leader
And a salt man of the earth.
Near the earth, he was we know
Standing only five feet four
But anyone tackled by Bobby Kellard
Always came out bruised and sore
His son Rob was often told by fans
'your dad was a dirty player'
"No, he was just a little bit 'ard," said Rob
"He always tried to play it fair."
He started out with Southend United
Then was signed, by Palace boss Dick Graham
And in midfields throughout the football world
Bobby Kellard caused sheer mayhem.
Combative, ferocious, tenacious
Were descriptive words for Bobby
Whose ruthlessness in winning tackles
Was on par with Mackay and Nobby
Sold by Palace to Ipswich town
Was the man with the chest of barrel

Once Upon a Rhyme in Football

Bought by Bristol City, Pompey,
And then Leicester's Frank O'Farrell
He re-signed for Palace in '71
About forty grand we paid
And after half a dozen games
Our captain he was made.
He led us into battle
Saved the team from relegation
Loved by all the Palace fans
For his inspirational dedication.
He wasn't a Martin Peters
And he weren't no Johnny Giles
But to the fans of Crystal Palace
He brought happiness and smiles.
Then transferred back to Pompey
He made the history books
First player ever sent off on a Sunday
After throwing a few right hooks.
So Bobby you were a rare one
A captain through and through
While some players for brekks have cornflakes
It was nails that you would chew.
So from all the clubs you rambled
And all the grounds you played
The name of Bobby Kellard
Will never, ever fade.

One thing for sure, the likes of Norman Hunter or Bobby Kellard would not be fans of the VAR (Video Assistant Referee) system that has been implemented in the modern game. After the first couple of seasons of use it's obvious that it needs some serious tweaking. It's pathetic that the duty VAR man can spend ages checking every angle before finally disallowing a goal because a player is a fraction of an inch offside.

Some changes to the game down the years have been good. Goal line technology has been almost perfect. Goalkeepers being forbidden to pick the ball up from a kicked pass back has worked favourably in keeping the game flowing. The ref's spraying that shaving foam stuff, to make sure the players stay back ten yards at a free kick, has curtailed a lot of cheating. Then Powers that Be ruin it all by making both the offside law and the guidance for what constitutes handball totally undecipherable. Meanwhile the introduction of VAR has completely slowed the game down. Nothing worse when your team scores than knowing you must try and keep your emotional celebrations on hold. All you get is the chance to sing "This aint football anymore," while the VAR man – like the Bletchley Park codebreaker in World War Two— is locked down at some secret address, deciding if you should cheer or cry. So, who is this VAR man who gets to watch over all this football and make all these life-changing decisions? Here's a little spoof on him.

BOB – THE MAN FROM THE VAR

Bob sat in his mum's furnished basement
Watching re-runs of *Murder She Wrote*
And on to a small piece of paper

He wrote to himself
A wee note.
"Remember to change over the channel.
Make sure you do it by Three.
The suits at the VAR head office
Want me watching the games on TV."
So Bob plugged the Var recorder
Somewhere in the back of his telly
Then went and made up some sarnies
With pastrami to fill up his belly.
As he lay on the couch he put up his feet
And waited for the Var official to call
Was someone offside?
Did some player dive?
Or did somebody handle the ball?
But the games all seemed to lack action
There was nothing for old Bob to note
In fact he got so bored with the football
That he turned back to 'Murder She wrote.'

John J. O'Connor

Meanwhile up in the North-East of London
In the fancy and new White Hart Lane
Spurs fans are all dancing and cheering
And singing the name Harry Kane
He's put Tottenham ahead
With a nice little play
But the refs called it back,
To Tottenham's dismay.
He got a signal from his linesman
Saying he thinks it's offside
So the ref calls a pause
So that Var can decide.

Bob was watching the adverts
When the phone call arrived
"Quick look at Spurs-Watford!
Do you think Kane was offside?"

So Bob views the footage
It's a tough one to settle
So he decides the best thing
Is to put on the kettle.
As he sips on his cuppa
And dips in a bickie
He still thinks deciding a decision
Is desperately trickie
He checks all the angles
With a compass and rule

Once Upon a Rhyme in Football

The first time he has used them
Since he was in junior school.

Meanwhile back in North London
The crowd is in a state of uproar
As both sets of fans sing
"It ain't football no more."
Conte on the sideline is going insane
And it looks like the Spurs fans
Will smash White Hart Lane.
Now Bob checks more camera views
To help with his mission
But after twenty-seven close-ups
Has still no decision
He presses pause on the camera
To put Kane's right foot on still
He's either on or offside
By one eighth of a mil.
Finally Bob grabs an old sovereign
To toss in the air.
Heads would be offside,
And tails it was fair.
The old ways are the best ways,
When all others fail
Thought Bob as he picked up the coin
That was showing him a tail.
The scoreboard showed "Goal!!!"
And Kane slid on the floor
Exactly thirty-two minutes

John J. O'Connor

After he drove home to score.
The fans they cheered wildly
And sang of their star
And Conte smiled slightly
And later praised VAR
At half-time Bob called in a sickie
Said he had stress and sore throat
Poured a nice big hot toddy
And turned back to '*Murder She wrote.*'

I suppose one day we'll all get used to VAR and wonder, as with Google, Twitter, and Face Ache how we ever lived without it. Still to this day, there are arguments about whether England's third goal in the 1966 World Cup final should have been allowed. The VAR man, with the technology he nowadays has at his disposal, might have been able to put that one to bed after a quick review.

Another event in the following World Cup in 1970 is probably one of the most reviewed pieces of action in the history of football. It wouldn't have needed VAR. Why? Because there was absolutely no controversy. It involved Pele, arguably the greatest footballer in the world at the time, and England goalkeeper Gordon Banks, who was rated by many as the world's finest netminder. A powerful header from the Brazilian was heading to the bottom corner when Banksy managed to get across his goal and flip the ball over the bar. Many regard it as the save of the century. What it needed and received was countless television replays at every possible angle to try and answer the question the whole world was asking. "How on earth did he make that save?

THERE'S ONLY ONE BANKSY

When millennials hear of Banksy
They think of the bloke who scrawls on walls.
But when oldies think of Banksy
They recall the great goalie saving balls
And his heroic days at Wembley
Especially in July of Sixty- Six
But it's four year later we'll remember more
The star between the sticks

John J. O'Connor

It was a hot and humid afternoon
Beneath the scorching Jalisco sun
When Banksy made the greatest save
That's been bettered since by none
The great Jairzinho got the ball
He was on the right wing for Brazil
And he took on Terry Cooper
With the score line still nil – nil
He went 'round Cooper skillfully
With confidence and ease
Then heard a cry, "On me 'ead son"
Yelled in guttural Portuguese.
He sent the cross in powerfully
And Pele's head it met
And everybody watching thought
The ball was in the net.
GOL !!! screamed Pele excitedly
As he raised his arms with glee.
"Pele puts Brazil ahead"
Said the man on ITV.
But Banksy on his near post still
Was having none of that
He hurled himself across his goal
Like a circus acrobat
He got his hand beneath the ball
After allowing for the bounce
"The greatest save I've ever seen"
The TV expert now announced.

Jairzinho eventually broke the deadlock
And Brazil won – one to nil
But that save by Banks from Pele
Is shown and talked of still.
Now Gordon passed away last week
He's moved to heaven from his grave.
And the first question that God asked him was
"How on earth did you make that save?"

Every football fan fell in love with that brilliant Brazil team of 1970. Twenty-six years later in 1996 every English fan was infatuated with the England team in their quest to win that year's European Championships, which were being held in England. It was the start of the "Football's Coming Home" era. After three seasons in existence the Premier League was really beginning to take off and establish its brand. Sky Television poured money into the product and average footballers were receiving financial rewards way above their wildest dreams.

The Chattering Classes were another infiltrator of the Beautiful Game in that era. Historically they were more drawn towards cricket and rugger. Football was the domain of the working classes. But in 1996 they started appearing in numbers at football grounds around the country.

Fair play to them, they stuck it out and nowadays, with the price of football so outrageous, it is really only people who take home higher – than – average wages that can afford to attend the games on a regular basis. I know Nouveau fans have received his or her share of stick about their lack of passion, but hey they are here to stay. So as far as I'm concerned, they're entitled to a poem.

I hope any fans reading this who think they might fall into this new category, will realize that this piece is written with tongue firmly entrenched in cheek.

THE NOUVEAU FOOTBALL FAN

He doesn't swear at the referee
Or question who's his dad
The nouveau fan has come along
Cos it is the latest fad.

Once Upon a Rhyme in Football

He always followed rugger,
He played it while at school
But when footer came home in '96
He found it 'ooh so cool.'
Nouveau owns a season ticket,
There's no problem with the dosh
And his accent is a mixture
Of urbanite and posh.
His home's a trendy town-house,
In an area once run down,
Usually along the River Thames
Or near to Camden Town.
His home library is extensive
In knowledge he is rich
But the only football book you'll find
Is Nick Hornsby's 'Fever Pitch.'
Of '66, he thinks of Hastings,
Or the year of his favourite wine
But "They think it is all over"
Is his all-time favourite line.

Nouveau worships Tony Blair,
And Frank Skinner floats his boat,
And he compares Pele with Socrates
'Cos of his 'BEAUTIFUL' football quote.
The FA Cup's a no show, or any game it's wet
And he won't stop off on the way to the game
To place a little bet.
No stopping in the local pub

John J. O'Connor

And with the die-hards have a brew
No nouveau likes to be in his seat
By twenty-five past two.

His stat knowledge is incredible
He'll tell you how long Zaha had the ball
But he's never heard the Roker Roar
Or been to the Old Den at Millwall.

His feminine side comes shining through
When the opponents score a goal
And when the TV camera zooms right in
It's the cue for his tears to roll.

He shouts at Gallic players in French
To impress those sitting near.
But when his team scores a winning goal
He'll hardly raise a cheer.
He'll stand up and politely clap
Then sit down like a lamb
And leave with half an hour to go
To beat the traffic jam.

Some readers you will think
This is nouveau discrimination
But he's just a sad by-product
Of a Sky Sports World generation.
It matters not he hasn't witnessed
The sloping pitch at Yeovil
'Cos when the novelty starts to wear
He'll be watching cricket down the Oval.

I hope that last piece wasn't too hard on poor old Nouveau. In his (her) defence modern football is a much safer event to attend these days than it was in the not-too-distant past. Nowadays, you can attend an away game, cheer for your team, wear the team's colours and have a reasonable chance of not getting your head handed to you by some yob who's had a tough week on the factory assembly line.

This wasn't always the case and away fans tended to keep their colours well hidden. This didn't always guarantee their safety. Clothes were a big clue to someone's geographical abode; Londoners, for instance, tended to be more fashionable than their northern chums, some of whom seemed to be living in a time warp when it came to their wardrobe. Also, accents were a dead giveaway of your place of origin.

One of the many back alleyways in Moss Side, Manchester. Attribution: ALAMY

Home fans were notorious for asking the time to fans they suspected were not from the locality. It was extremely hard to fool a native. Unless you were a skilled linguist there was a fair chance that after your weak attempt to impersonate Arthur Scargill, at somewhere like Leeds, you'd soon be putting in your best effort to break the 200 meters sprint record. Occasionally you didn't get the chance and you'd find your sorry self having to take one for the team. One of the most fearful places for away fans was Manchester City's Maine Road. Nestled in between run-down terraced houses and intimidating alleyways, the ground was situated in the notorious Moss Side area of the city. Being away alone at Man City was no joke.

AWAY ALONE AT CIT-EH

My mate called me frantically,
via telephone,
Telling me I'll have to travel,
To Man City all alone.
Gave me some excuse
I'm sure he'd just made up
Same as when we drew Millwall
Away in the cup.

Callaghan was Prime Minister,
Slade and Sweet the bands
And when you travelled away alone
You took your life into your hands.
I went to football matches, minus any malice
All I wanted to do
Was to follow CRYSTAL PALACE.

Once Upon a Rhyme in Football

So on the Saturday morning,
I say goodbye to the wife
Hoping to return that evening
With victory and my life.
I exit the M6 the journey's gone to plan
And the first person that I see
Is a young Man City fan.
"UP THE PALACE !!" I bravely shout,
At the lad, who's about nine,
And speed away up the road
As he gives me the V-sign.
I park a mile from the ground
To be on the side of caution
But straightaway I become the victim
Of local mob extortion.
"It's twenty-five pence mate,
so no one cuts yer tyre
and another twenty five
so yer car don't go on fire."

In London he'd be told to F-off and get lost
But when you're travelling away alone,
It's all part of the cost.
I looked around at the terraced street
And thought of Coronation
As I gave the little bastards
Their 50 pence donation.

I notice jean-clad city hoodlums,
Hanging out in pairs

John J. O'Connor

Checking out the strangers
With confrontational stares.
I didn't have my colours on,
It was something that was taught
Only wear a scarf away from home
If you've thousands in support.
It's alright for the Chelsea's,
The Everton's and the Pool,
But to wear my Palace colours
I'd be a bloody fool.

Still three hours to kick-off,
I've got some time to kill
Maybe a couple of pints of ale
Will help my nerves to chill.
I ask a friendly copper
Where I can get a peaceful drink
And he rubs his chin in thoughtfulness
And at his colleague gives a wink.
"Ooop the road lad, make a right
you'll find a nice saloon.
It's perfect for away fans,
It's called the 'Old Blue Moon'."

Into the public house I go,
It's a mass of City blue
And a hundred hostile faces thinking
"Who the hell are you?"
I squeeze my way up to the bar
Afraid of being vocal

Once Upon a Rhyme in Football

One wrong word out of my mouth
And they'd know I'm not a local.
I know a London accent
Would be their excuse to start a fray
Oh how I wished I'd stayed at home
And never went away.
The pub was loud and noisy,
As of their heroes they did sing.
Of Colin Bell and Rodney
And Tueart upon the wing.
They sang they hated Forest
And Man United too
These were the rougher elements
Of the City crew.

The barman had an Irish face,
And an Irish brogue that matched
And when he asked what did I need,
A cunning plan I hatched.
"Oyl have a point of Guinness."
I asked in an Irish twang
And I stood my ground till half past two
Until last orders rang.

"He's just some Paddy who's got lost,"
I heard a patron say
As any attention on myself
Seemed to go away.
It was nearly time for kick-off,

John J. O'Connor

And as I walked out of the bar
I was grabbed by a City bruiser
Whose face it bore a scar.
"Hey, you Irish bastard .
Don't come in here no more
And this is for the Birmingham bombs,"
he growled,
As he knocked me to the floor.

I decide my safest action,
Is to make a fast retreat
And I find myself beside the ground
On a place called Kippax Street.
Then in my utter confusion
I did something I didn't intend. . .
I entered the nearest turnstile,
Into the City end.

The game kicked off, with
"COME ON CI-TEH"
Echoing in my ear
As I stood there frozen in my spot,
Too terrified to cheer.
City scored before the break
And the Kippax end went wild
And I clapped my hands politely
And very falsely smiled.

Then in the final minute,
Don Rogers made a break

Once Upon a Rhyme in Football

And he left a trail of City players
Chasing in his wake.
He rounded big Joe Corrigan
And tapped it in to score
And in the City end
I could contain my joy no more.
I excitedly jumped up and down
Joyfully punching air
I was signing my death warrant
But I didn't really care.
A thousand fingers pointed
Chanting my head would be kicked in
For I was a Cockney in the City end
And that was a mortal sin.

They surged down the terraces
Telling me my destination
Even kindly letting me know
The form of transportation.
I took a couple of glancing blows
As they moved in for the kill
But then thank God I was rescued,
By a handful of 'Old Bill'.
They took me by the arms
And led me from ground
Escorting me through the back streets
Until my car was found.
I slumped into the driver's seat
Of my faithful Morris Minor

John J. O'Connor

And looking in the mirror saw
I had a whopping shiner.

Once back on the motorway,
I let out a mighty sigh
As I looked back at grim Manchester
Where I'd thought I'd die.
It was not long after midnight
When I got to face the wife
"For God sakes, John,
what have you done,
why don't you get a life?"
So, for a week I groveled
And took care of her needs
Then two weeks after City
I was driving up to Leeds.

Once Upon a Rhyme in Football

I know my generation loves nothing more than a good old moan about how much better the game used to be. We nostalgically tell stories about how we were terrified out of our wits at away games. We make cult figures out of players who should have been serving time in Wormwood Scrubs or playing for their local pub team, not making a living as a footballer. We hail as tactical geniuses managers whose half time pep talks amount to, "hoof it oop there lads!" We reminisce about muddy pitches, slide tackles and. . . Okay, I'll stop there, I'm getting a little teary eyed here. In defense of Nouveau and the modern game, what I'm getting to is that there have been many plusses brought to the matchday experience in the last 25 years or so.

One of the things that sprung up in the 90's was the pub quiz. Much of the time the topic was just football and all the saloon soccer experts could test their wits against their mates and the quizmaster. Unfortunately, just as video killed the radio star the introduction of mobile phones, texting and bloody Google have pretty much destroyed the pub quiz. Just as a pub dart league gave variety to the week, there was nothing like a Tuesday night quiz down the local. Here's a ditty about those nights.

John J. O'Connor

FOOTBALL QUIZ NITE

It's football quiz night down the pub,
Which year did England introduce the sub?
Such are the questions players would face
Would they earn some street cred,
Or find disgrace?

The four contestants are raring to go
To raise their hands they can't be slow.
There's Charles the student
With his scarf and glasses
Bill the stat man who counts shots and passes.
George McPhee, who hails from Fife
And hen-pecked Steve hiding from the wife.

Bob the landlord reads the first question aloud,
"***What football match had the record crowd?***"
"1950 in Brazil, over two hundred thousand,"
Shouts out Bill.
"Point to Bill, let's carry on
Who in football was called 'The Don'?

No whispering answers you lot at the back
If you need a clue he played in attack."
"Don Rogers of Palace is 'The Don' I know"
"Well done Charles, ten more to go.

Four teams in the league
whose name ends in 'E'?
Please don't answer if you've only three."

Once Upon a Rhyme in Football

Bill's hand goes up
And he says with a smile,
"Crystal PalacE and Plymouth ArgylE."
"You didn't listen, I said I need them all
You were much too quick
for those names to call.
There are two more teams – please don't fail,"
And Charles jumps up and shouts "Port ValE."

"Well done Charles,
But now the boys have three
So it's up to you Steve
and George McPhee."

Steve's deep in thought
As he sips on his ale
Brain working overtime
'til it reached Roch – dalE.

"Rochdale," Steve shouts,
"Where I first met 'er indoors.'
I should have gone instead
To the Yorkshire Moors."
"Okay, Steve, let's not get personal!
Who in 1970 managed Arsenal?"

They are all deep in thought
As if in a trance
As they work their way back
From the man from France.

128

John J. O'Connor

"Your time is up lads,
I'm going to ask McPhee,"
Who, caught unawares, asks,
"Do you mean – me?"
"Great stuff George, don't sound surprised
Bertie Mee managed, that great Arsenal side.

Now a letter in the alphabet
that only one team has got?
It could be an English team,
Welsh or Scot."

They try for an X —- Z and Q,
But finally give up,
'cos none of 'em knew.
"The answer is Saint Johnstone
and the letter it is J "
says Bob to the players',
And the crowd's dismay.

"Last English manager to win the Prem?
No one gets this answer
it's a bloody gem."
Stevie answers "Wilko,"
But the answer it was not,
And Bill thinks it was Fergie
But is informed that he's a Scot
All four contestants
Reluctantly throw in the towel

And Bob the questionnaire
Lets out a mighty howl.

"I knew no one would get it,
and the answer makes me sick
'cos no Englishman has won it
the question was a trick."

After the final question, all four are tied at three
Now it's time for a well-earned pint
And a quick dash for a pee.
For Bob has a tie breaker
To see who knew the most
So the winner could sit down in the pub
And of his football knowledge boast.

"Right then lads, may the best man win
And no conversing with the crowd
And all you rowdies at the bar
Please no whispering names aloud.

The midfield 'School of Science'
I know the name was unofficial
But I want you to give me their surnames
And their first name's first initial."

"Charlton, Law and Best," says Bill
"I know the answer's in that vicinity"
"No you silly fool," laughs Bob
"That's United's 'Holy Trinity'."
"S. Heighway and B. Hall," says Charles

John J. O'Connor

"I heard they were better than Wayne Rooney."
"They were the school of nowt," growled Bob
"They were famed for going to Uni"
"Cunningham, Regis, Batson,"
Is the answer of McPhee's
"No" said Bob, "you're well off there
they were West Brom's 'Three Degrees.'"

It's up to you now Steve," says Bob,
As the pub punters roar him on
And he comes up with C. Harvey
And H. Kendall of Ever – ton.
Steve knows there was a third one
His brain strains at the test
As he goes through that Evertonian team
Starting with goalie Gordon West.

But suddenly the pub door bursts wide open
And in storms Stevie's missus
And she's not there to declare her love
Or shower his face with kisses.
"If it isn't bloody football
It's cricket, darts or pool!!
And I'm up at six each morning
To bring our kids to school."

But the only school in Stevie's mind
Was the Evertonian School of Science
So, deep in thought he ignores his wife
In a clear act of defiance.

"I'm at home with the kids
you don't even think to call.
I'm watching Corrie on my own
While you're out having a — ball."

"A – Ball?" cries Steve, coming out of thought
And the crowd all raise a cheer
And at that moment what he'd said
To him becomes quite clear.
"Well done," said Bob,
"You got it right, Kendall, Harvey, Alan Ball,
you win a night's free drinking
of your favourite tipple, Skol."

"Oh no he's not – he's had his fun
He's coming home for grub"
Says Stevie's wife dragging him out the door
End of Quiz Nite down the pub.

So Alan Ball, the final answer, was another great English footballer who was taken way too early. One of the finest midfielders of his generation, he will be fondly remembered for his high-pitched voice, his flaming red hair and the trademark flat cap he always wore during his later managerial career.

He was a Blackpool player in 1966 when, at the tender age of 21, playing for England in the World Cup final at Wembley, he ran the West German defense ragged. Many observers rated him man of the match. Although Sir Geoffrey Hurst might have something to say about that.

After the World Cup he joined Everton and became part of the legendary midfield "School of Science." I think that despite his moves to other clubs and the fact he had two spells with both Blackpool and Southampton, most neutral fans, will associate him primarily with the blue of Everton.

He was transferred to Arsenal from Everton in 1971 for a then record fee of 220,000 pounds. He moved to Southampton in 1976 and also spent a few seasons playing in the North American soccer league, before his playing career wound down at Bristol Rovers. He then took the plunge into management. Bally, like a lot of players, got the early call from " the man upstairs."

HAVING A.BALL IN HEAVEN (Early Call for Alan)

There's a knock – knock – knock
On heaven's gate
And St Peter takes a peek
Sees a feisty little red head
Then hears a voice that starts to squeak.

"Any chance of coming in?
My name is Alan Ball"
St Peter says, " just wait a bit
I'll go give God a call."
A minute later Pete returned
Saying, " you're more than welcome – lad
Your place is there – on that cloud
Right next to your dad."

Then Pete strolled off to do his thing
And God came walking by
And to the little redhead he did apologize.
"Things ain't been too good up here
That's why you got the early call
Our teams are lacking passion
They required an Alan Ball.
You'll be playing for us on Saturday
We're playing Paradise at home
You'll be in your favorite position
In front of Mooro and Labone.

"Harry Catterick and Sir Alf will coach
They've formed an unholy alliance
Since you played with Ramsey's
wingless wonders
And Harry's 'School of Science.'

"The Saints will sing, 'Go Marching In'
As your fans did at the Dell
And the Pompey chimes will ring so loud

John J. O'Connor

They'll hear them down in Hell.
The Arsenal Gunners will give salute
To your deeds for the Highbury cause
And all across the clouds of heaven
You'll be given much applause.

"But the greatest sadness down on Earth
Will be on the blue side of the Mersey
Where Evertonians won't forget
How you proudly wore their jersey.
They'll serenade you with the chant
    'The King is Alan Ball'
    And they'll grieve and cry
      And wonder why
    You got the early call."

Keeping with the A Ball theme the next piece is about the object that keeps millions of folks throughout the world entertained, happy, excited, angry, sad and many other emotions besides. It's the noble orb itself, our favourite all-round friend, the leather football, which surely deserves a poem of its own.

But let's not be too sympathetic when giving our revered kick-buddy its due. The football can be a cruel companion. Anyone who back in the day ever headed that muddy blob of leather will tell you with a cringe that if your head ever connected with the lace then you had a memento tattooed to your forehead until you used your dad's sandpaper to scrub it away. Also many's the up and coming young star who spent nights worrying about the chances of ever becoming a father after (pre-ticky-tacky days) a team mate blasted a five yard pass straight into his unmentionables.

There is also overwhelming evidence that constant heading of the ball leads to degenerate brain disease. I recall the latest finding is that an ex-professional footballer has three – and – a – half times more chance of getting a brain related illness than regular Joe Public.

So to prove it's not just the modern day human who likes to play the victim, here's an ode to our leather clad friend.

FOOTBALL VICTIM

I've been kicked outside in all kinds of weather
"Don't worry about her,
she has skin that's like leather."
I've been kicked hard with insteps
Side – foots, and back – heels

John J. O'Connor

And none of you can know
Just how bad all that feels.

The abuse it starts usually
Sometime in the week
And then, on a Saturday reaches its peak.
Head-butts connect, squarely on my round face
And at times I retaliate with the knot of my lace.
I've been called fifty-fifty and told I am loose.
I don't know how I put up with all this abuse.

Being kicked almost senseless to me is no joke
Especially the pain of a vicious toe poke.
I'm swerved, curved and punted,
Passed all around
And men dressed in black
Drop me, down on the ground
I've been bounced, thrown, and flapped at
And used to show tricks
And I recall a bad kicking from Julian Dicks.
Men wearing gloves punch me up in the air
Life for this victim just ain't very fair.

Once Upon a Rhyme in Football

I sometimes get kidnapped
When I land in the crowds
And at Watford and Burnley
I would hide in the clouds.
At places like Arsenal
I'm just used to pass
And when I complain
I get a kick in the grass.
Some like to dribble me, others to trap
And I've been violently hurled
By a bloke called Delap.
I've been shot, I've been floated
I often get robbed,
I've been kept as possession,
And I sometimes get lobbed.
I bend and I dip
Make the lads think they're good
Then just to annoy them I bounce off the wood.
I've been half-volleyed and squared
Flicked on and chipped
And over the bar I'm frequently tipped.
I've been caressed by Brazilians,
The Argies and Dutch
And the Spaniards are fond
Of a very quick touch.
But the women all hate me
They say I have sinned
They rant that I'm only an old bag of wind.
They do their comparisons,

John J. O'Connor

Brand me a threat
'Cos their men love them less
Than me in a net.
Also I've been waterproofed
So now move very fast
But I still get abused
Like I did in the past.
So next time when you see me
Being violently kicked at a wall
Remember I'm a victim
JUST A POOR LITTLE BALL.

As a fan, in the past, it was easy to become a victim at football. Inside the ground – or outside — you were prone to danger. However, despite some of the dangers, one of the great positives you got as a travelling fan was the geographical knowledge gathered along the way. Yes, a stern geography master could tell you where Timbuktu or Madagascar was, but did he know how many miles it was from South London to Darlington? Would the learned man have known how many exits you had to pass on the M1 from London before you stopped at the Watford Gap service station for a well-earned jimmy riddle stop after the effects of the Watney's Party Seven's had started to play havoc with the kidneys? No, he would not.

GEOGRAPHICAL FOOTBALL

We'll start at Great Ian Britton
It will only take a while
Alan Sunderland, Jon Sheffield
And ex – Palace Wayne Carlisle
Joe Bolton of Sunderland
John Aston of Man U
Geoff Barnet for Arsenal,
Cup Final – Seventy two.
Jamie Clapham, Alan Devonshire
Alex Stepney, Kevin Poole
Doing all this geography
Is like being back in school.

Chris Sutton, Matt Derbyshire
And Luton's Alan Slough . . .

John J. O'Connor

We've travelled all Mike England
It's time to leave it now.
We'll just make a very quick trip
To the city of Dwight Yorke
Then head Gordon West across the sea
To the County Alan Cork.
Joe Mayo, Dion Dublin,
Stephen Ireland and Shaun Derry
And Chelsea striker Dixon,
Whose initial name was Kerry.

Rob Douglas on the Isle of Man
Then ex-Liverpool Sean Dundee
Jason Scotland, Justin Edinburgh
And the gracious Bob Paisley.
A quick visit to the Valleys
And Gareth Barry Town
And then we're on the plane again,
Milan Mandaric bound.

Once Upon a Rhyme in Football

Then Joe Jordan in the Middle East,
Matt Holland by the Dams
Alan Brazil by the Amazon
And Alan Durban of the Rams.
In Texas, Stewart Houston;
A problem* we have got
Bryan Hamilton in Ontario,
Who else have I forgot?
Oh yeah — Asa Hartford in Connecticut
The last stop on the trip
I'm going to sail a boat home now
And test my David Seaman-ship

---

* "Houston – we have a problem". For those of you who never followed the space programme..*

When Crystal Palace players left the club in the 70's they didn't need to have an international grasp of geography. All they needed to know was how to get to East London. Once there they could ask a friendly passerby or policeman how to get to Brisbane Road the home of Leyton Orient.

Palace seemed to be a feeder club for Orient in those days. At times the O's fielded as many as six ex-Palace players. Unfortunately for Palace they sometimes fed the O's with players who still had a bit of hunger about them – and while Palace slid down to the old Third Division, Orient thrived and assembled a team that just missed out on promotion to the top tier.

TO HELL OR TO ORIENT !!!

'Twas way back in the day,
Many full moons ago
Crystal Palace had their own knacker-yard.
To send players who'd slowed
Who no longer glowed
And who were finding Division One hard.

It was over in grimy East London
On the no-go-at-night Brisbane Road
And for many a player
Who was worse for the wear
It became their playing abode.

To Hell or to Orient!
Would cry old Bert Head
In his best dictatorial voice

And the player would know
It was his time to go
And in the matter, he had little choice.

See George Petchey had left Crystal Palace
Where he'd been the side kick to Bert Head
And he took over the reins of the Orient team
The East Enders who played in the red.
So the O's got the likes of Phil Hoadley
Mark Lazarus, Bill Roffey, John Sewell
The East Londoners rose
With all those old pro's. . .
George Petchey was nobody's fool.

Even fan favourites were auctioned
To oil up the Orient machine
John Jackson, Whittle and Possee
David Payne and the great Gerry Queen.
Yes, the mid-Seventies were horrid for Palace
Life in the Third just wasn't much fun
But when Orient needed players
We flogged them our spares
And they nearly ended up
With promotion to One.

But most Palace supporters were happy
That all their ex-players did so well
They were proud of the men
Who'd transferred to East 10
A postcode just better than hell.

John J. O'Connor

So thank you all those long-gone players
Who gave fans of both clubs
So much pleasure
And as the old adage goes
It certainly shows
One team's trash
Is another one's treasure.

It was a fairly common practice for players to wind down their careers at lower- level clubs. Even greats such as Bobby Charlton and Bobby Moore ended up playing in a lower division. In some cases, players would find themselves back at the club where they started out. For many Scottish players this meant taking the trip back north of the border to where, many years before, they had left with just a pair of boots and a dream. Adapting to life in the real world had to be faced once final performances were played and the beaten up body couldn't give any more. There were only so many coaching positions in football, so usually this meant the ex-players managing a newsagents or more likely going into the pub trade. It was here that they could happily regale customers with their many tales of days gone by.

John J. O'Connor

A LITTLE PUB IN SCOTLAND

I returned up north of the border
To finish my football career
And like many a player of that era
Became a publican serving up beer.

Now's many a night up in Scotland
When the door of the pub I must close
I'll feel just a wee sentimental
So I'll keep in the punters I know.

I'll pour me a wee glass of whiskey
And let my mind go a wandering back
And I'll reminisce to the after-hours drinkers
About my days in the Tottenham attack.

I'll tell of my goals v United
Signed by Spurs as a youth from East Fife
And the discos and clubs of North London
Where I had the best times of my life.

And while I feel a wee tear on my cheekbone
As my mind wanders back forty years
I wish I was back in North London
Nae, in Lanarkshire serving up beers.

Talking of occupations many of our surnames came about because of the work our forefathers had to do to keep grub in the cave, castle, condominium, or wherever it was they lived in bygone days. Here's a few footballers whose surnames give a hint at what skills their ancestors might have possessed in order to keep the wolf well away from the main entrance.

FOOTBALL OCCUPATION

Adopted from our forefathers' jobs
Came many a given name
So let's check out some footballers
To see past claims to fame.
For the man who Phil Parkes your Willie Carr
You'll never beat Paul Parker

John J. O'Connor

And the man who imitates your dog
You've Wolves' old Ritchie Barker.

Did Spurs' Paul Miller really work
In the Yorkshire Danny Mills?
And did Mark Nurse of Swansea City
Dish out medicine and pills?
Peter Taylor patched your pants up
Joe Baker supplied your bread
Terry Butcher chopped your pork up
And Phil Barber shaved your head.
Kingsley Black and Tommy Smith
Fixed your horses' hooves
And Stuart Slaters ancestors
Worked high up on the roofs.

The Walsall Saddlers, they made sure
You had a comfy seat
And Barry Silkman made the purses
For the rich elite.
The Evertonian Toffee men
Make sweets that children like
And the Crewe Alexander Railway Men
Taught the world how to go on strike.

Kevin Pressman pressed your trousers
Or did he write the news?
And the Northampton Cobblers
Did very well by your shoes.
Was David Seaman in the navy

Once Upon a Rhyme in Football

Working on the ships?
Did Tony Waiters take your orders?
And work hard for his tips?

Gordon Marshall took care of crime
With the help of Denis Law
Paul Mariner would catch your fish
And sell them to you raw.
Chris Coleman delivered black stuff
To keep you warm in winter
And Palace star George Wood
Was always wary of a splinter.
So, here's to all our ancestors
And all the jobs they did!
And if you think of this rhyme as childish
I never mentioned Brian Kidd.

On the topic of names, remember when you could name nearly every team off by heart. It used to be pretty much the same twelve each week. No complaining from the players about having to play two games in three weeks and moaning in the same breath that they don't get enough match-time. Nowadays it's hard to keep up with the twenty-five-man squads and a different team put out for each competition. I believe the company line when a top team gets knocked out of one of the cups by a lower-level team is: "We put a team on the park that we thought was capable of winning the match."

Also, with so many imports it can be hard to remember all the player's names. You've multi-lettered Russians, Portuguese aliases, and unpronounceable African names to contend with. Personally, I find the most annoying thing is the multitude of hyphenated names that have appeared all over modern footballer's shirts. I understand that these days especially, a lot of marriages end in divorce. But this new fad of also sticking mum's name on the shirt is so unfair on the terrace lyricist. I dread to think what it will be like in another generation, when some already hyphenated kids' marriage dissolves and his offspring becomes a footballer demanding three surnames on his shirt.

ELIMINATE THE HYPHENATE

When I came of footballing age
Hyphenated names were not the rage.
Well there was one — Ian Storey-Moore
A much longer name than Denis Law
Alan Bloor or Ian Ure.
But it was rhymer-friendly
A terrace lyricist's dream

Once Upon a Rhyme in Football

And would trot off the tongue
As you cheered on your team.
Stiles to Best – Best to Law
Out on the wing to Storey-Moore.

Then one day off springs of Ian Wright appeared.
Both good players who defenders feared
But the name Wright-Phillips
Didn't roll from the tongue
So neither ever heard
Their names being sung.

Now footballs in the midst of its latest craze
Names like Oxlaide-Chamberlain
And Villa's Jake Doyle-Hayes.
Ruben Loftus-Cheek and Brooklyn Lyons-Foster
If you pay for every letter on the shirt
I'd imagine it will cost-ya.
Try putting a tune to Hal Robson-Kanu
Or Cameron Humphreys-Grant
I'll bet you all your Esso coins that you bloody can't.
So when players get bored of this fad
And sling their hyphens from the pram
They'll have to think of another way
To honor dad and mam.
So no disrespect to James Ward-Prowse
He'll understand I'm sure
But football life was so much simpler
With just Ian Storey-Moore.

John J. O'Connor

As young fans going to Selhurst Park, one of the names we had a problem getting our tongues around was that of Missus Minchella. She was the hard-nosed, tough-as-nuts, elderly lady who sold peanuts to the peckish masses and held legendary status among the Selhurst Park faithful. If a game wasn't going well for the home side and the crowd fell silent, you would still hear the cry "PEANUTS FORRA SIXPENCE – A TANNER A BAGGA!" from Missus Minchella. The Palace peanut seller was a private woman, but some of the mystery surrounding her has come to light in recent years. So first the rhyme, then the further revelations.

MRS. MINCHELLA
(The Palace Peanut Sella)

Some called her Lou – Lou, some Isabella
But to most fans at Palace,
She was Missus Minchella.
"PEANUTS FORRA SIXPENCE
A TANNER A BAGGA!"
Her accent went through you
Like a sharpened-up dagger.
She was boisterous and moody
And prone to a moan
And before Kane was to Tottenham
She was one of our own.

Back in the Sixties and Seventies
Her primitive bark
Would compete with the chants

Once Upon a Rhyme in Football

At pre-match Selhurst Park.
"One, two, three, four
Can you hear the Palace roar?
Peanuts for Sixpence"
Would mock the visiting fans

Unlike the players who came, played, and went
Missus Minchella was always there
Rain, snow. wind — sun or hail
You'd always hear her accented wail
   "PEANUTS FORRA SIXPENCE
     A TANNER A BAGGA!"

So who was the mysterious Missus Minchella?
The monkey-nut lady with the feisty demeanor
The bandanna covered head
And the olive-skinned leathery face.
A face that had memories it couldn't erase.
A face that witnessed poverty, war, relegation
A lined face that saw sorrow
But not much elation
Many claimed to know her,
But no-one really did.

Urban legends abounded
Some said she was an Italian countess
Who fled the Nazis
It was also whispered
She had Mafia connections.
That in her younger days

John J. O'Connor

Was a raven-haired beauty
Whose husband died on war time duty.

That the large gold earrings
Hanging down to her shoulders
Would fetch thousands if sold.
Some assumed she was a gypsy
Who hoarded her gold
In a secret compartment
That her basket would hold.
That she lived in a mansion of luxury
Far away from the din,
Of match-day Selhurst Park
From her boisterous persona and thunderous bark.
   "PEANUTS FORRA SIXPENCE
      A TANNER A BAGGA! "

Some bought her wares
For a quick pre-match snack
Others to take aim
At the stern Peeler's back.
If your aim was well practiced
And your nut hit the cop
You felt like Jocky Wilson
Finishing on double-top.
She was hated by police
And the ground staff alike
The apprentices on Monday
Felt like calling a strike.

Having to clear more spent shells
Than a Baltimore street
Shells that had been stomped
By thousands of feet
That throughout the match
Had jumped up and down
With an occasional knees up
To old "Muvver Brown."

On terraces packed,
Kids being passed to the front
Missus Minchella for sales
With her basket would hunt.
She'd wade up the terrace
Basket tied to her chest
Sometimes assisting the coppers
To make an arrest.
Parting the red and blue sea
Of working class humanity
As easily as Victor Moses would part
The heart of an opposition defense
Many's the decent pre-match terrace brawl
Was rudely interrupted by the threatening call
Of Missus Minchella.
"Stoppa you punching,
you kicks and head butts!
Putta you hands in your pocket
and buya my nuts."
They always did.

John J. O'Connor

She pulled a crafty substitution
In Seventy-One.
Decimalization meaning
We changed up our mon.
She subbed the D for the P
Said it was just doing her job
And so our cherished monkey nuts
Cost just under a bob.
But she still said tanner.
  "PEANUTS FORRA FOUR PENCE
    A TANNER A BAGG!"

One mid-football season
Around the year Eighty-Four
At Palace Missus Minchella
Was not seen anymore.
At first no one took much notice
But soon with the rumour mill
We got a bad vibe
Was Missus Minchella dead
Or was she alive?
She was murdered by the Mafia!
She was banned by the club!
But all of these stories just didn't add up
Nowadays, "Find Missus Minchella"
Facebook groups would spring to life
And Twitter pages would be rife
But then there was just gossip.
More than a Coronation Street corner

Or a Sky studio on transfer deadline.
She was reported seen, at the Den, Millwall
And selling nuts at the Albert Hall
At a Status Quo concert at Charlton's Valley
And even outside the Hammersmith Palais.
She was sighted at Sainsburys
More times than Elvis
But sadly — never again at the Palace.

Now the tannoy makes the pre-match noise
As fans stare at their phones
Oblivious to the sounds of Elton

Mrs Minchella the peanut sella

John J. O'Connor

And the Rolling Stones.
But old timers claim to hear another sound
As they moan 'bout peanuts for two pound
They swear that as the game gets near
A voice attacks their inner ear.
After maybe drinking too much Stella
They claim to hear the voice of Lou-Lou Minchella
And despite the tannoy blaring out
The latest sounds of Lady Gaga
They hear the feeble, eerie cry
"PEANUTS FORRA SIXPENCE
A TANNER A BAGGA."
The ghostly voice of Missus Minchella
The Crystal Palace peanut sella.

At Selhurst Park it wasn't just players and managers who became legends. In the 70's alone we had Clive (Sideburns) the programme-seller. . . Len Chatterton (The Flatter) the groundsman who, at half-time used to drive his car on the pitch to flatten it. We also had Hy Money, our glamourous female photographer and Joyce the Voice, a supporter whose vocal support could be heard from one end of the ground to the other. While the Voice urged the players on and questioned the parentage of the ref, her husband would sit quietly at her side.

As for Mrs. Minchella, everyone who went to Palace in that era remembers her fondly. A newspaper article a few years ago cleared up some of the mystery that had surrounded her. She was born in Italy. Her disappearance from Selhurst was due to a new chairman who it was said, wanted a bigger cut of her profits. The club denied it had anything to do with her departure. It's said she told the chairman in exactly what location of his anatomy she would like to place her peanut basket.

She was the mother of six. She never learned to read or write, had limited English and lived in a Victorian house not far from the ground. One day her husband, Ralph told all the kids not to argue with their mother and walked out — never to be seen again. His daughter Josephine assumes he went back to Italy. "Every day," she said, "when my mother went out with her basket she went out hoping to find him."

After Palace, Mrs Minchella continued selling her wares every day, out of her pram, in the Croydon area. Unfortunately, some geniuses, in their infinite wisdom, designed underpasses in Croydon that were a paradise for muggers. Three times Mrs. Minchella was mugged. Each time she fought back. The last time they got her wedding ring and tore her earrings off and beat her badly. She was hospitalized for some time. When she came out of hospital her family intervened and forbade her from going out selling nuts. Poor Mrs. Minchella died in a nursing home in 1991 at the age of 82. According to a nurse she used to wander off a lot, walking the streets for hours, still looking for Ralph.

* * * *

Football fans are a needy bunch. They want match programmes, they want Bovril, they want peanuts. During the 1975-76 season what the faithful at Selhurst Park demanded most was "Whittle."

Alan Whittle a fan favourite, spent a fair amount of time that season out of the line-up or on the subs' bench. If things were not going well for the home side it wouldn't be long before reverberating around the ground was the the chant of "We want Whittle!"

A group of Palace fans even bought a racehorse that they called "We want Whittle."

"WE WANT WHITTLE"

"WE WANT WHITTLE" came the cry
From the four sides of the ground
And during that dismal season
It was the loudest sound around.

It was the season of '75 that ran into '76
And the crowd would scream for Whittle
To come on and show his tricks.

We were languishing in the Third that year
And the fans all felt dejected
Especially when their favorite player
Wasn't being selected.

Alan Whittle gliding past Peter Rodriguez of Southampton in the 1976, F.A Cup semi-final at Stamford Bridge. Attribution Keith Payne photo (clubs official programme photographer)

"WE WANT WHITTLE" would start off low
Then reach a rousing din
As everyone convinced themselves
We needed Whittle there to win.

Alan Whittle — signed from Everton
Was a blond-haired dynamo
But according to Big Mal Allison
Was not always the perfect pro.

He dropped him to the subs bench
And sometimes to the stands
But when Whittle waved up to the crowd
Thousands clapped their hands.

John J. O'Connor

Liverpool had their super-sub
And Villa had Brian Little
But their fans never begged as much
As we did for Alan Whittle.

"WE WANT WHITTLE!" came the cry
From all sides of the ground
And at Selhurst Park that season
It was the loudest sound around.

Even forty-five years on
When old time fans get bored
The 'WE WANT WHITTLE," chant goes up
To show he's still adored.

That was an example of a football crowd demanding, trying to force the manager into doing something that they deeply wanted. Nowadays their passion is usually vented towards the Chairman or owners as they chant for the manager's head because the team has drawn two matches in a row. Blackburn Rovers fans were a clear example of fan-power, or bullying, when, in 2012 they forced manager Steve Kean, into resigning. At the time of his parting the team was lying in third place in the Championship. What though, when it's the other way around and the Chairman forces his wishes onto the fans?

In 2010, Forest Green chairman Dale Vince banned all meat products from the ground and in 2015 Forest Green became the first all-vegan club in the world.

Bet the old time chairmen, some of whom ran chains of butcher-shops are still rolling in their gravy. Of course, the British public will take these changes with a little moan down the pub, then except that fad word 'CHANGE' and let the new breed of owner dictate to them how they should conduct their lives. I could imagine the uproar if an owner tried to ban hot dogs or burgers at an American football, or baseball arena. It would not be pretty.

By the way, this piece was written when Rob Green was playing for the Hammers, so I hope the seventeen people who'll end up reading this book don't bombard me with e-mails telling me that he is now earning a living as a pundit.

HAM – BURG 0-0 WEST – HAM

"You can't sit here, you must sit there."
Football's become too much to bear.
Stewards yelling, "Stay in your seat"

John J. O'Connor

Chairmen dictating what we must eat.
You can't eat meat, or have a smoke
The game has now become a joke.

*For some strange reason the Forest Green owner
thinks this sort of food is bad for you.*

The numpty on the tannoy
Tells fans when to sing.
The fans are puppets on a string.
Soon they'll tell us, we can't drink beer
"God forbid if the natives cheer."
Chairmen worried for our health
Sell all-organic and up their wealth.
The name West Ham they'll take away
But the goalie's Green so they'll be okay.
No industrial language for that is bad
No asking the ref does he have a dad.
No telling the linesman he needs new gogs
No steak and kidney, or large hot dogs.
Games postponed 'cos of a little ice.

Once Upon a Rhyme in Football

We took Sky's money
Now we've paid the price.
Yes, the way the things are,
Be very afraid
'Cos the game's now run
By the prawn brigade.

John J. O'Connor

In the owner's defence, eating too much meat has been proven bad for the old cholesterol. But what about when they ban something that has been proven to improve your quality-of-life healthwise. For many years Chelsea fans had a ritual whereby they would come to games armed with celery sticks. Being a naughty bunch, they were known on occasion to hurl the salad veg onto the playing area. Finally, in 2007, the club banned fans from bringing the healthy accessory into the ground. It also encouraged fans to use a special hotline to report those they thought were bringing the green stick of veg to the footer. Joey Stalin would have been so proud.

DIRTY TRICKS AND CELERY STICKS

They came for my fishing rod
But I do not eat fish
They asked where my hounds were
I said fox ain't my dish.

They came for my cigarettes
I said,– I no longer smoke
They asked where my booze was
I said,– I drink Pepsi or Coke.

They came for my dustbin
But I always recycle
They were looking for car fumes
But I travel by cycle.
They looked on my bookshelves
But there were no books to see

But then they went to the kitchen
And found my celery
THAT NIGHT THEY CAME FOR ME.

Seeing as we're on a health kick at the moment, let us get back down to the farm and the last part (thank God says you) of Football Farm. This one is called "Football in the Water."

FOOTBALL FARM (Part 3)
FOOTBALL IN THE WATER

Down the Gordon Hill we go
Past Gerry Ryan's daughters
Looking for the football stars
Who play in the Joe Waters.
We see 'Fowler is Cod'
Sprayed on a whitewashed Peter Wall
Then have a quick kick about
With a bouncy Alan Ball

We go along the Gordon Banks
Just by the old Paul Lake
And make ourselves Alan Comfort
As observations we try to take.

Once Upon a Rhyme in Football

We see young Peter Haddock,
Or Addicks we should say
'Cos that's the slang for haddock
Down Sarf London way.

Pretty Swans from Swansea
With Ralph Coates of David White
Heads bobbing proudly,
Eyes darting left and Tommy Wright.
Geoff Salmons of Sheff United,
Going with the flow
And, as he did at Bramall Lane
Putting on a show.

Shrimpers swimming Frank-Swift -ly
Trying to avoid the net
And the infamous Peter Swan
Is trying to place a bet.
Mariners from Grimsby searching for a catch
But they're relying on Dave the Seaman
So there's not much chance of that.

Skillfully avoiding tackles
Is Charlton star Mark Fish
Who doesn't fancy being the food
On anybody's dish.
We spot a tearful crocodile,
Which makes us all excited
And we're informed by the Saints Hugh Fisher
That it supports Dundee United.

John J. O'Connor

So as we stand here on the Richard Shaw
The wind turns to Tony Gayles
And soon enough the heavy rain
Turns into Derek Hales.
So our adventure comes,
To its final halt
It's over and David Dunn
And as we head back to reality
I hope you all had fun.

Once Upon a Rhyme in Football

There's a good chance that when you think of fish, you either think of the thing that went with your chips after the pubs shut on a Friday night, or you think of Grimsby. That is (for anyone who opted out of Geography or lives beyond Britain) the nice little, much maligned trawler town situated by the North Sea in the Northern part of England.

Then when you think of Grimsby your mind conjures up images of football matches taking place on wet and windy Tuesday nights. Why? Well because every lazy journo who has ever covered football will always use the cliché, 'a miserable, rainy Tuesday evening in Grimsby.' After reading this line for about the 783rd time recently I decided I had to spring to the defense of the much-ridiculed Tuesday night football match.

GIVE TUESDAY NIGHT A BREAK

To all you football scribblers
A promise can you make
When writing about a football match
Give Tuesday night a break.
You describe atmospheric Wednesday nights
At Tottenham's White Hart Lane
But a Cup thriller on a Tuesday night
Is treated with disdain.

Scouts don't watch players on sunny days
In Rio or in Rome
No– it's always on a Tuesday night
Wet, hungry, far from home.

John J. O'Connor

Seems like everyone plays Grimsby
On a rainy, Tuesday night
And the scribes make this a cliche
Almost every time they write.

Yes, the purists love their Wednesday match
Cold nights are 'crisp and cheery'
But mild nights up north on Tuesdays
Are described as "cold and dreary."

So I'm not trying to be no Tennyson
Nor even William Blake
I'm just trying to say, "Come on you guys
Give Tuesday night a break!"

A ll this talk of cold, fresh air in Grimsby, celery sticks and fish, sounds ever so invigorating. Seriously though, how many footballers from the golden era would have wanted that menu to eat? Very few it seems. A big steak and a large serving of greasy chips was the order of the day for those starving athletes. It surprising though, that despite them liking a fry up and consuming industrial amounts of ale, the vast majority of the players from that era were fairly slender in build. Not a Nautilus manufactured muscle in sight. Totally different from today's muscle bound, ink covered, super athletes, who spend their down time counting calories instead of pints.

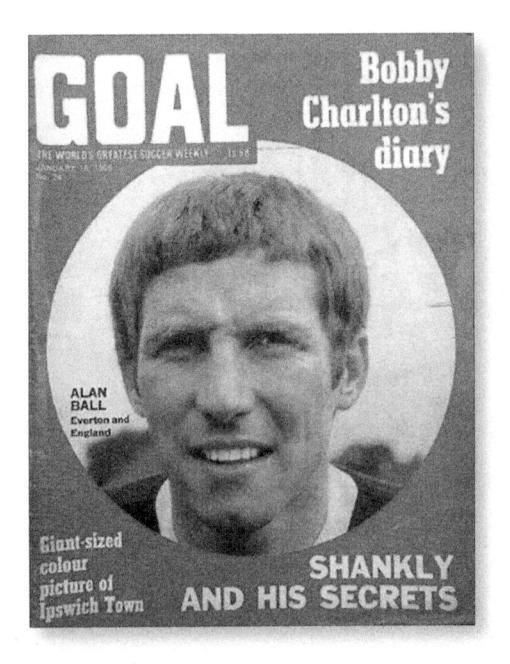

Does anyone remember *Goal* magazine? It was in circulation for six years from 1968 to 1974. At its high point its weekly sales were nearly a quarter of million copies. It was eventually incorporated into *Shoot* magazine. In every issue of *Goal*, a current player was profiled. It pretty much followed the same format of questions.

I thought that, just for a bit of fun, it would be interesting to compare the answers the players of the past gave, in comparison to what I think would be the answers from the modern player. Modern players' answers are in bold.

PLAYERS PROFILES
(Past and Present)

QUESTIONS:
NAME?
> OLD PLAYERS — Willie, Stanley, Bobby.
> **MODERN PLAYERS — Jermaine, Darren, Robbie.**

Q. WHERE WERE YOU BORN?

Dagenham, Glasgow, Durham
Left home in me early teens.

LAGOS, PARIS, ROME
AND LOVELY MILTON KEYNES.

Q. WHERE DO YOU LIVE?

A terraced house in Croydon
not far from the training pitch.
I'd like to live out further
but I'll never be that rich.

A ten-bedroomed Tudor Mansion
In Wilmslow or the Wirral
Surrounded by ten acres
With foxes, deer, and squirrels.

Q. MARRIED?

Yes, to the girl I went to school with
Who also lived next door.

**Live with my baby's mother
For how long I'm not too sure.**

Q. FAVOURITE FOOD?

Steak and chips, and the Sunday roast
And in the morning beans on toast.

**Pasta, Pasta, farm fresh fruit
Creatine powders and ginseng root.**

Q. FAVOURITE DRINK?

Lager, milk, and pints of stout

Designer water—cleans toxins out.

Q. FAVOURITE HOLIDAY DESTINATION?

Devon, Blackpool, Margate
A trip to the Brighton Pier
We never won promotion
So can't afford no trips this year.

**My private beach in Cyprus.
My posh Sardinian villa.
Disney World in Florida,
For the kids it's quite a thrilla.**

John J. O'Connor

Q. MOST INFLUENCE ON YOUR CAREER?

Got to be the gaffer you know
You know – You know…
He gave me old man twenty quid
And signed me, well you know.

My agents had a massive influence
But I've now a massive moan
He got me a massive contract
But now I'm out on loan.

Q. DO YOU ENJOY BANTER WITH THE FANS?

On my way up to the ground
I meet them on the bus.
They wish me well and clap me
And generally, make a fuss.

I run to them at the end of games
Hands clapping above my head
But when they ask me for my autograph
It's something that I dread.

Q. WHO ARE YOU CLOSEST TO IN YOUR LIFE

Just to keep the peace
I'd better say the wife.

My bodyguard and minders
They're the ones who save my life.

Q. WHAT DO YOU HATE MOST ABOUT AWAY TRAVEL?

The eight-hour trip to Cumbria
And far off destinations
Trying to hold the pee in
Till we reach the service station.

Queuing at the airport,
For our eight-minute flight to Stoke
Unable to use our mobiles,
The whole thing is a joke.

Q. WHO DO YOU FEAR MOST?

Nobby Stiles, the taxman
The gaffer, Dave Mackay.

The News of the World and People
They're after me on the sly.

Q. FASHION ACCESSORY?

My big red jar of Brylcream
To help me part my hair.

Milan designer clothing
And a model who is fair.

Q. TOUGHEST THING ABOUT TRAINING?

Returning after three months off
And sweating off three stone.

Practicing goal celebrations
And diving on your own.

John J. O'Connor

Q. WHAT DO YOU DO AFTER TRAINING?

Up to the nearby bookie
Then off to the local pub.

**Open up my own wine bar
And soak in a nice steam tub.**

Q. MOST PRIZED POSSESSION?

A Duncan Edwards autograph.
My only England cap.

**My cell phone and Ferrari
And the computer on my lap.**

Q. WHAT WOULD YOU DO IF YOU WEREN'T A FOOTBALLER?

Down the mines with me dad
Try and learn a trade

**Model or a dee – jay
So my talents on parade.**

Q. WHAT ARE YOU GOING TO DO WHEN YOU RETIRE?

Maybe coach the juniors
Or buy a little bar
Have to work on the docks again
Cos my savings won't go far.

**Write my fifth auto-biography
And host my own chat show.
Trade in my ageing partner
And enjoy my well-earned dough.**

Q. FINALLY LADS WHERE SHALL I DONATE THE MONEY FOR THIS INTERVIEW?

To the children in Biafra
It is a truly worthy cause

To my testimonial dinner
Where I'll receive deserved applause.

A player profile question that Goal magazine liked to use was, "Who would you most like to meet?" Occasionally the likes of Frank Worthington would give us a laugh by saying something like, "*the bloke who broke into my car.*" or "*the wag in the crowd who cries 'Windy' every time I hoof the ball away.*"

But apart from the humorous comments it was surprising, in these less spiritual times, how many players said they'd like to meet the Pope. Or if a player was asked what other hobbies he had, he might say that, after church on Sunday, he would head over to the local golf course.

Religion has always been hovering around football. Differences between Celtic and Rangers are well documented, but there was also quite a history of religion and politics behind the scenes at clubs like Manchester United, Tottenham and Everton.

One of the little life lessons people are taught is that you never talk about politics or religion in a saloon. Well, this ain't a pub, so I'm going to have a little go at mixing football and religion.

The Anglican Church, St. Lukes is surrounded on two sides by Everton football club. The statue is the midfield school of Science, Harvey, Kendall, Ball. Photograph courtesy of Rob Sawyer.

MIXING FOOTBALL AND RELIGION

Football is a religion,
To that we all agree
And if this upsets the bible belt
To leave now they are free.

We'll trek towards St Mary's
Where the Saints have marched on in.
Just me and a few of the Masses,
Off to repent our sins.
We enter the Derek Temple,
And at a Dave Cross make the sign
Then Phil Neal down at a Graham Pugh
And ask for peace and John Devine.

We see born-again Christian Daileys,
With slogans on their chests
'Jesus Arellano Saves
but Remi Moses he invests.'
Ian St John pops his head in
But very quickly leaves
And someone's yelling after him
"Where the hell is Greaves?"
We see little Maradonna
Looking fit and tanned
Goal hanging around the alter
Waving someone's hand.

John J. O'Connor

We enter the confessional Tommy Booth
To replenish all our sins
And pray that all our games this year
Will end as handsome wins.

We see Juan Pablo Angel
Floating up above.
And listen to Ian Bishop
Preaching peace and love.
Don Rogers walked on water
But we don't see him around
And David James is scared of crosses
So he's nowhere to be found.

We see a very Jason Priestly looking
Evertonian Dixie Dean
And Sister Teresa Niall Quinn
As he was called by Man U's Keane.
The Tony Book of Genesis
By Owen Archdeacon is read aloud
And Nicky Pope of Burnley
Waves to the surging crowd.

We see three Dennis Wise men
Plus Mark Lazarus and Frank Saul
And a picture of Jimmy Gabriel
Up on the Ben Abbey wall.
We notice all the mini-gods
Like Kenny and Henrikk

Once Upon a Rhyme in Football

And big Jim Cannon tells us
The Earth will be inherited by the meek.

The lesson is, if we live by it,
Then we'll die too – by the sword
Thundered down from the Roy 'Evans
By Burnley's old Bob Lord.

So we leave the Ivor Allchurch
Vowing to live on Mark Fish and bread,
Looking forward to opening day
And the 40 weeks ahead.

Football certainly was a religion to a lot of my generation growing up. We lived it, drank it, ate it, slept it and most of all dreamt it. Our dreams were usually the sort where we'd become the next George Best. Or, for those of us with less lofty goals, the next John Sewell. "Who the hell's John Sewell?" I hear some readers ask. Well, if you ever watched *The Big Match,* on a Sunday afternoon in the early 70's, you'd know. A hoof by Shovel (as he was affectionately known) into the box went through the hands of Leeds goalkeeper Gary Sprake in the last minute of a league match at Selhurst Park in 1970. It was shown for at least a year afterwards in the introduction of *The Big Match* show. The fluke goal gave Palace a 1-1 draw and Sewell a place in Selhurst folklore.

Sewell, the club captain, looked anything but a professional footballer. Always immaculate, even on a muddy pitch, it was said he looked more like a bank clerk than a sportsman. He wasn't a fan favourite, nippy wingers in the top flight tended to give him the runaround——but that goal against Leeds changed all that. John finished up his career in the United States, then went into coaching. Later he ran an English teashop in California called 'Awfully civilized.' Sadly John passed away at the end of 2021.

JOHN (THE SHOVEL) SEWELL
an awfully civilized defender

He resembled a middle-aged bank manager
Not a team captain from that era
But to all of Crystal Palace fans
He was our Bobby Moore or Shearer.
His name was John (the shovel) Sewell
And his position was right back
A crisp and tidy tackler
Who often moved up in attack.

Signed from neighbours Charlton
For an eleven thousand fee
His debut was v Bristol Rovers in October 63.
The fans they called him 'Shovel,'
Which they shouted with devotion
And his finest moment came in '69
When he led us to promotion.

He was only ever booked but once
When he accidentally clipped a heel
But Bert Head wrote in for leniency
And the FA granted his appeal.

However ——that equalizing goal v Leeds
Is what the Palace hordes remember
As he latched onto a pass from Scott
Who was filling in for Kember.

"HOOF IT IN THERE! "screamed the crowd,
As in the box he sent her
And if Sewell had been Brazilian
You'd have sworn to God he'd bent her.

The ball hung lazily in the air
And took a little swerve
And poor Gary Sprake in the United goal
Seemed to lose his nerve.
First he thought to punch it
Then he went to catch
And he made a total cock-up
Of the last kick of the match.

As the ball with elegance gained the net
Selhurst Park let out a roar
And the Shovels' name was safely set
Forever in folklore.

Yes, we soon got to realize that all those football dreams were just that—dreams. But what happens later, well into your middle years when you're still having footballing dreams at night. Sad, I know. Trouble now is—that without the innocence of youth and with all your years of worldly experiences, these dreams can sometimes turn sinister. Here's a poem called "A Dream of Two 'Alves," which I'm blaming on either cheese sarnies before bedtime or some bad ale down the local gin palace.

A DREAM OF TWO 'ALVES

I dreamt I was back in late 60-something
Being driven down Wembley Way.
Waving to the cheering fans
Along with Eddy Gray.

I dreamt I met with Mooro,
For a flutter and a beer
I was hitting all the nightclubs
With Osgood and Kinnear.

I dreamt of exchanging passes
With Summerbee on the flanks
And of the forty-five-yard curler
I put past Gordon Banks.

I dreamt I was a Busby Babe
And a Celtic Lisbon Lion
And that I was worshipped up on Tyneside
As their greatest number nine.

John J. O'Connor

I dreamt of saving penalties
And scoring winning goals
Turning defenders inside out,
Alongside Marsh and Bowles.

But as I tossed and turned in sleep
My dream it took a turn
And instead of looking like Georgie Best
I looked like Rodney Fern.

I dreamt the crowd all booed me
Each time I touched the ball
And I dreamt I wore my colours
In the wrong end at Millwall.

I dreamt I nutmegged Vinny Jones
Who wasn't one bit pleased.
He told me in no uncertain terms
That his studs would find my knees.

Once Upon a Rhyme in Football

I dreamt I played for Liverpool
And roomed with big Ron Yeats
And all the hotels—where we stayed
Were owned by old Ted Bates.
My dream then went fast forward
And I got another fright. . .
I dreamt I got the managerial post
At the Stadium of Light.

But then I heard an alarm bell ring
And I woke up in a sweat
Just as me and Rooney
Were about to place a bet.

So as I dragged my body to the shower
And pulled across the curtain
I prayed that on the other side
Stuart 'Psycho' Pearce wasn't lurkin'.

Most people never realize their dreams, but some have fun attempting to fulfill them.

I know a lot of old-time players may sound envious of modern players and their huge financial rewards, plus the first-class facilities where they train – and play. But I'd bet my old pair of Peter Bonetti gloves that they had a far more enjoyable career than the modern player. Back in the day the players would train for a few hours, three or four days a week. Now it's all play/train/play and no fun.

But there were also plenty of players from the past who found their dream only to see it eventually turn into a nightmare. What inspired the next poem was Cristiano Ronaldo, a few years back describing how a footballer was the equivalent of a slave. Many ex-pros, who had never had the chance to earn the riches that Ronaldo and his ilk earn, were rightly peed off. As of course were the millions of people working their butts off all week in the hope that at the weekend they might have the price of watching the slaves perform.

AN OLD EX-PRO'S LAMENT

They say a footballer's life's is slavery now.
God!—I wish I felt their pain
Like I did when tackled from behind
The reason I walk now with a cane.

Cortisone became my drug of choice.
It helped me play each game
Little did I know back then
It would eventually leave me lame.

Once Upon a Rhyme in Football

Flair was the strong point of my game
All swerves and shoulder dips.
But now I have the price to pay
As I wait to get new hips.

We roasted our defenders
No twenty-five-man squads.
And when we reached our sell-by dates
It was back to docks and hods.

Metatarsal was near Sunderland
Well that's what we'd have thought
And every high ball in the box
By our keeper it was caught.

We defended both our goalposts
We had men out on both wings
And when we saw fans on the bus
They treated us like kings.

We charged nowt for an autograph
We were privileged just to sign.
We all just thanked our lucky stars
We weren't working down the mine.

A beach ball wasn't used back then
And we weren't scared of the mud
And yellow cards weren't given out
For every little thud.

John J. O'Connor

There was no such thing as diving
Or tearing off our shirts
And no running crying to the ref
When you got kicked where it hurts.

We played for love of the game
Money wasn't the only reason
The most I made in a playing year
Five grand in my last season

Local folks still buy me drinks
They still recall, v Spurs, my goal
But every Thursday afternoon
I still sign on the dole.

So as I line up in the solemn queue
With some characters unsavory
I wish I was playing in the Prem
As a part of legal slavery."

The final three poems are all family orientated. The first one, "The Old man and his Grandson," is a fictional piece that shows the difference in how the generations view the beautiful game. The second one is about how my mum killed Bobby Charlton (no — wait till you get to it) and the final one is a tribute to my late father, the great Pat O'Connor, who along with my mum knew absolutely nothing about football.

THE OLD MAN AND HIS GRANDSON

In a northern mining village
That politicians helped destroy
A Grandfather meets his Grandson
Who's no more a little boy
The Grandson's a millennial
Born the year of ninety-five
And grand-dad's nearly ninety
And just barely alive.
The Grandson loves his football
And his heroes Scholes and Shearer
Granddad loves his football too
But from a very different era.
The Grandson hails from London
And for a few days he is staying
With Granddad way oop North,
In a house that's now decaying.

The old man rolls a ciggie
Then makes a cup of tea

John J. O'Connor

And asks his young grandson, politely,
Would he turn on the TV.
"Here, put this old tape on for me
You young ones have the knack
It will show you real footballers
And what nowadays they lack."
The young lad eyed the cover up
When he pressed video to play
It was all about the football game
From way back in the day.
As they made themselves comfy
And then turned up the sound
The Grandfather smiled
And the young fellow frowned.

They watch Man U v Benfica
Eintract Frankfurt – Madrid
Celtic 'gainst Inter
And Giles, Gemmell and Kidd
They view Finney and Blanchflower
And many more from the past
But the Grandson just observed,
"They don't look very fast.
Do you know Zaha runs a hundred
In nine point nine-secs?
And no one hits a football like Shearer or Becks."

As the lad kept on talking
He watched Charlton with the ball
Who cracked one from fifty past Willie McFaul.

Once Upon a Rhyme in Football

"Now that's how you hit 'em lad
That was some mighty thud!
And look at that football all covered in mud."

"Look at that pitch
And those two-footed tackles"
said the Grandson, who then added,
"Stiles should be tied up in shackles"
The grandfather smiled
His eyes glistening with glee.
As he watched Norman Hunter
Chop down Franny Lee.
They watched Greaves play for Tottenham
A player whom the lad didn't think much
"Greaves strolled through that game,"
He said, "hardly getting a touch.
Do you know Kane runs for Tottenham
Seven-point-three miles a game?
It doesn't look like Greaves
does anywhere the same."

"You weren't focusing thy lad,
You were lookin' at thy phone.
Jimmy Greaves scored four goals there
All made on his own."
They watched Lee, Bell and Summerbee
And clips of George Best
While the young lad checked Facebook
Not one bit impressed.
"He was drunk on the pitch,

John J. O'Connor

But just look at his pace."
But his Grandson just shrugged, and said,
"he's an absolute disgrace.
Do you know that sports scientists,
to a man, nearly all insist
It takes a week to recover
if you go out and get pissed?"

"Aye lad, I do hear you,
but he was the best player alive. . .
I don't know if you noticed
in that match he scored five."
They watched Mortensen and Matthews,
Peters and Hurst
And a scorcher from Lorimer
When the net nearly burst.
They viewed Gilzean and Nat Lofthouse

Once Upon a Rhyme in Football

Jim Baxter and Law
But the grandfather's grandson
Was not the least bit in awe.
"They all look so slender, so dainty, so thin
And they all have their socks
Rolled way down on their shin.
Their bodies lack muscle – no ripped definition.
Not enough pasta, creatine or nutrition."

"Believe you me young lad
Them there were tough times
When I worked with the hardest men
Down in the mines.
Those players they got kicked
But nowt did complain
And not one of them dived
Or did injury feign."
The grandson he argued
His generation's more strong
And his grandfather offed the telly
And told him he's wrong.
He took a pull on his ciggie
His lungs starting to pant
His face reddened up
As he started to rant.

"You can stick your metatarsals
And your Health and Safety looneys
All your foreign coaches,
Your Pogbas and your Rooneys

John J. O'Connor

Keep your snooker-table pitches
And those blow footballs that you use
Bring back the old characters
who liked to gamble and to booze."

Then out of the blue
There was a mysterious sound
As a plaque with a medal fell onto the ground.
The grandson retrieved it,
From the carpeted floor
And when he read it,
He knew he'd slag Grand-dad no more.
The engraved medal read

Arthur Suggett June 6, 1944
For your Gallantry when you fought
on that cruel Norman shore
And for the bullets that you took
and all the lives you did save
This medal made for heroes
goes to the pick of the Brave.

"How awesome!" said the Grandson,
"I had no idea you were a hero."
As he straightaway forgot
About Scholes, Beckham and Shearer.
"It's nowt, thy lad," said Granddad shyly,
"It's only a piece of metal.
Now put that stupid phone away
and stick on thy bloody kettle."

The penultimate (I've been dying to use that word) poem is about my dear mum who is still alive and dancing at the tender age of 92. She never followed football. . . which was good in some ways.

I remember once, after a game being chased along my local High Street, by some rather un-sporting Leeds United fans. My mother was just coming out of the butcher shop as I went flying past her in my best impersonation of some young sprinter auditioning for the Munich Olympics. Those beer-bellied Yorkshiremen didn't have a chance of catching the nimble young athlete I was in those days. However, surviving the angry Leeds fans was one thing; explaining to Mum why I was legging it down the crowded street with a gang of burly, older men running behind me was another. I decided to come clean and tell her the truth. I told her that after matches home fans and away fans have races among themselves. She was happy with my explanation and allowed me to go to the next match.

Luckily, she was blissfully unaware of the disorder that occurred at football back then. Mind you that didn't stop her committing an act of unforgivable violence in my upstairs bedroom on a late September night back in 1970. (There might be a song in there somewhere)

Me and my mate were playing Subbuteo; a game which was responsible in that era for keeping thousands of young tearaways off local street corners. It could occupy the attention of a youngster for much longer than the ADHD pills the doctors started dishing out a decade later to day-dreamy adolescents.

When you think of it, we weren't that much different from some of the kids today. We old timers are always moaning about the young generation having their heads stuck to mobile phones, or wandering around like zombies with wires protruding from their ears, looking for some object called Pokemon. But there we were in the 70s spending our youth flicking little plastic men around on the floor when we could have been doing our algebra homework or cleaning out the coal bunker.

We organized our Subbuteo games like professionals. We took the outcomes very seriously—but unfortunately on that late September night my mother just didn't realize the importance of the event taking place on the carpet in the upstairs bedroom. While my mate and I got ready for our own Cup Final, we had no idea of the traumatic event that was about to unfold.

THE NIGHT MY MUM KILLED BOBBY CHARLTON

It was a late September.
Not as far back as Sixty-Three
Much more near the year Seven-tee
All day at school I was in a dream
Trying to figure out my team.
As the history teacher ranted on
About ancient Greece and Rome.
All I cared about on that day
Was getting to my home.

It was around seven o'clock that night
When my mate came round
And we prepared the green velvet
To act as our ground.
This was our Wembley,
On my bedroom floor
And as lads of eleven

We could wish for no more.
Subbuteo cup rounds
We'd played through the year
And now the conclusion
Was desperately near
The last two teams standing
Must play for the crown
Manchester United against Ipswich Town.

A quick cup of char
Then before we can start
We make preparations
For looking the part.
We have four small lit-up floodlights
For a true atmosphere
And a couple of terraces
Where the fans can all cheer.
A referee and two linesmen
And some other props
And to ensure law and order
We station two cops.
The players lined for the anthem
Both teams in a row
Then we set the alarm clock
And off we did go.
We sussed each other out at first
Like two tactical masters.
But Alex Stepney in United's goal
Let in two disasters.

John J. O'Connor

Man United pulled one back,
By whom I'm not so sure
And equalized soon after
With a lob from Ian Ure
We swapped ends at the half
And took a little break.
Then started up the game again
With everything still at stake.

The play got quite aggressive
I complained of Ipswich fouling
Then I bravely brought on Sadler
For slow-moving Alan Gowling.
It proved a stroke of genius
As he put Man U ahead
And after fifty-two minutes
It was still three-two they led.
But Ipswich tied it up, right bang on the hour
When Viljoen fired past Stepney
With ferocious shooting power.
Now Ipswich pressed on forward
They were going for the kill
And they nearly scored another
Stepney saving from Mick Hill.
They camped out in United's half
As for the winner they did hunt.
While in the opposition half
I had Charlton alone up front.

Once Upon a Rhyme in Football

Suddenly the bedroom door pushed open
With the score line still three-three
There was my mum with sandwiches
And a couple of cups of tea.
"Take a quick tea-break, boys,
Before you ruin your eyes.
I've cups of tea, some sandwiches
And a couple of apple pies.
I'll leave them on the bed,
Now stop and have a munch."
And as she walked across the pitch
We heard a mighty *CRUNCH*.

If our final was being televised
Ken Wolstenholme would have to say
"Viewers at home of nervous disposition
kindly turn away."

John J. O'Connor

"You've just broke Bobby Charlton," I said
Before being stunned into total silence
Wondering how my dear old mum
Could have committed
This act of violence.
"Oh not to worry," said my mum,
"I know just what to do.
When I'm at the shop tomorrow
I'll buy that super glue.
They say it sticks forever
And never comes unstuck.
Now come on you boys, sup your tea
And into your sarnies tuck."

"But mum, that was Bobby Charlton
He cost me Five and Three."*
But all that my mum worried about
Was having us drink our tea.
"Ooh, you're right," she said, still smiling,
"Look at him,
he's even got a little shiny head.
Isn't it great what they can do these days."
As she placed poor Bobby Charlton,
Down upon the bed.
There was no stretcher for Bobby
Just the inside of Mum's purse

---

*On the off chance that someone under 60 reads this book, five (shillings) and three, about two days paper- round money in 1970, was the rough equivalent of 27p.

Once Upon a Rhyme in Football

Then he was whisked off to the glue shop
Without even the help of a nurse.
When the game did resume
My friend's laughter turned to howling,
Though he sportingly agreed he'd let me
Bring back Alan Gowling.
But now the spirit had gone from United
Their hearts weren't in the game.
Without their leader Bobby
They would never be the same.
My mate scored three unanswered goals
To put United six- three down.
And that year's Subbuteo final
Was won by Ipswich Town.

My mum she did get Charlton fixed
But the adverts were untrue.
Four minutes into his first game back,
He parted from his glue.
I put him in the bin that night
And felt a little numb
That back in late September
He'd been murdered by my Mum.

T he final poem of the book is a tribute to the greatest man I ever knew. My dad, Pat O'Connor, who sadly passed away in 2015 at the age of 83. He didn't have much interest in sports. He was too busy laying bricks and rebuilding a London Town, that had been bombed to bits by Hitler's Luftwaffe.

Despite his lack of soccer knowledge, he did like to be part of the football conversations, where his guaranteed input would be the announcement, "Now that George Best fella was a great fella."

NOW THAT GEORGE BEST FELLA WAS A GREAT FELLA (R.I.P. DAD)

In the middle of heated football conversations
Dad would butt in.
"Now that fella Best is a great fella,"
he'd say with authority.
Knew nowt 'bout football did Dad.
Where he was from, football was frowned upon.
The foreign sport, the garrison game
If you played it, you'd be banished
Either to the fires of hell
The pubs of Camden Town
Or to the Connaught Rangers.

Knew nowt 'bout football did Dad.
The muddy building sites of a London town
Ravaged by war, became his playing field.
Building became his game.

Once Upon a Rhyme in Football

He took to the trowel
Like Finney took to the ball.
He was passed bricks by hods
More than Hodd passed to Crookes.
Over doorways he built headers
Of which Astle would have been proud.
He knew more different brick bonds
Than Billy or James
And he built many brick arches
Alongside the Thames.
But he knew nowt 'bout football did dad.

Patrick O'Connor 1932 -2015

John J. O'Connor

When his sons started to play
He tried to learn the game
Although he never did.
But he did learn the name George Best.
"That George Best fella is a great fella," he'd say.
Interrupting the football intellectuals
As they discussed the intricacies
Of the offside trap
And the merits of a Terry Cooper overlap.

Not long ago dad had his moment of glory.
Some young Sky telly products
Were arguing in the pub
Was the greatest Ronaldo, Messi, Zidane?
And they all then agreed
Roy Keane was the man.
"That George Best fella," said Dad,
"Now he was some fella.
The greatest there was,
That I can tell ya."
A couple of old timers
Looked up from their pints.
Said one,
"There's a bloke who knows what he's talking about."
Dad grew in stature and rested his case.
A chuffed look of pride all over his face.
He knew his football did Dad.

Once Upon a Rhyme in Football

*George Best arriving at 10 Downing
Street for a dinner party in 1970.
Attribution– Popperfoto*

Now Dad's gone to heaven
In peace he will rest
And I'm sure he is mentioning
The fella called Best.
Now I don't know if George Best
Was a great fella or not
But when in his prime
Was the best of the lot.
But the one thing I do know
I'll tell you now, Dad
You might have known nowt about football

John J. O'Connor

But who gives two hoots?
Cos that fella Best,
As great as he was,
Wouldn't have been able
To lace up your boots.

Afterword

Okay folks, that's it. I hope you enjoyed the book and it brought back some memories. Thanks for reading and I hope that the team you follow got a mention. Obviously, some clubs got more exposure than others, but around 70 teams received some sort of acknowledgement.

If you'd like to read more of my football poetry you can find it at footballpoets.org/ or if you want to comment on the book (preferably positive, but I do have a thick skin) I can be reached at johpalcon@aol.com

Better still you could leave a review on Amazon.co.uk It would be really appreciated.

Next, I'd like to acknowledge all the lads and lassies who helped me make this book happen. A big thanks to you all.

Acknowledgements

Mike Berry
Helen Commisso
Liam Drew
Cliff Hopkinson
Peter Hurn
Natalie Jones
Angela O'Connor
Kevin Raymond
Rob Sawyer
Crispin Thomas
Ghislain Viau
Neil Witherow

About the Author

John O'Connor was born in Southwark, South London. When the family moved to the Croydon area, John became an ardent follower of the local football team, Crystal Palace. He has often wondered whether he'd have been a happier camper in life if the family had moved instead to Islington or Madrid. Then again, looking on the positive side he also realizes that they could have also ended up in Stockport or Accrington.

He continues to support Palace, but from across the Pond. In 1980, John went to the United States for a holiday and liked it so much he stayed. He settled in New York City and spent the next 40 years working as a bricklayer in the construction industry.

His first published work was the award-winning poem "The London Park Bench." It was published in 2001 and all proceeds went to the Aisling homeless center in Camden Town, London. Around this time John found an outlet for his football poetry via a web-site called footballpoets.org/ Up until the present he has had over 120 football related poems published on this site.

He has written numerous football articles and they have appeared in magazines such as BACKPASS-retro football magazine and Late Tackle. Some of his other works, mainly containing stories about life in the building trade have appeared in the magazine, Irelands Own, plus in newspapers, The Irish Post and The Irish Examiner.

John now lives in Nashville, Tennessee, and is currently working on a fictional football novel set in early 1970's Manchester.

Printed in Great Britain
by Amazon